ME POWER

ME POWER

LANYSHA T. ADAMS, PHD

NEW DEGREE PRESS

ME POWER

ISBN   979-8-88504-569-8 *Paperback*
979-8-88504-894-1 *Kindle Ebook*
979-8-88504-685-5 *Ebook*

Names: Adams, Lanysha T., 1984- author
Title: Me Power / Lanysha T. Adams, PhD.
Description: Washington, D.C. : New Degree Press, [2022] |
Includes Bibliographical References And Index.
Identifiers: ISBN: 979-8-88504-569-8 (Paperback) | 979-8-88504-
894-1 (Kindle) | 979-8-88504-685-5 (Digital Ebook) |
LCCN: 2022913076
Subjects: LCSH: Self-Actualization (Psychology) | Self-Esteem. |
Self-Perception. | Self-Realization. | Motivation
(Psychology) | Continuing Education)—Psychological
Aspects. | LCGFT: Self-Help Publications. | BISAC: SELF-
HELP / Personal Growth / Self-Esteem. | EDUCATION /
Philosophy, Theory & Social Aspects. | BODY, MIND &
SPIRIT / Inspiration & Personal Growth.
Classification: LCC: BF637.S4 A33 2022 | DDC: 158.1—dc23

LIBRARY OF CONGRESS CONTROL NUMBER
AVAILABLE AT HTTPS://LCCN.LOC.GOV/2022913076

To my parents, Janice Brewer, Jalisa Sanders,
David Foss, Davidson FiaFia, and Donovan Fatu

CONTENTS

APPENDIX

The privilege of a lifetime is being who you are.

—JOSEPH CAMPBELL

ME POWER:
AN INTRODUCTION

"The Admissions Committee regrets to inform you that we were unable to offer you a place in the doctoral program."

Reading my second Ivy League rejection letter, I thought, *WTF?* I was 90 percent certain I would be accepted. My prospective advisor Professor Obich and I had spoken several times, discussing collaborative research we could pursue. She seemed impressed and even invited me to join her doctoral-level seminar. Although everyone else had struggled to pass that class, I earned an A.

In an email requesting a meeting with Professor Obich, I wrote, "After reading your rejection letter, I came to realize some shortcomings in my application that perhaps I overlooked. Because I plan to apply again, it might be useful for me to better understand where I fell short."

I ran down two long, winding hallways that connected my office to Professor Obich's. At twenty-four years old, I had my own office in the building where Shirley Chisholm (the first Black woman elected to Congress) and John Dewey (pioneer of the learning by doing movement in education) spent time studying and teaching. I felt accomplished as a master's student and I looked forward to someday earning my PhD.

Before I walked into Professor Obich's office, I took a deep breath and reminded myself she would provide valuable guidance and feedback. I was facing a significant obstacle in my life, yet I felt prepared to do whatever it took to pursue my dreams of obtaining a doctoral degree.

Professor Obich welcomed me into her office, with her head cocked to the side and her coffee-stained teeth exposed. Sitting up straight, I opened my hands, signaling I was ready to receive feedback. There was no small talk and she immediately cut to the chase.

"We need to talk about why people like you aren't supposed to be in the program."

I held my breath, listening intently to every word. Professor Obich had taken the meeting to provide me with much-needed advice.

"You must be shocked by the fact that I said people like you. I meant it. People. Like. You," she repeated as she looked me up and down.

I pointed to my skin and she nodded.

"The work you do is very *applied*, LaNysha. My students and I only work in the surrounding community to receive funding, which allows us to conduct research and publish." I started looking around the room, thinking there were hidden cameras and someone would jump out shouting that I'd been *Punk'd*.

"Academic research and writing are not done by people like you because you're most useful doing applied work."

The more she talked, the more my shoulders hunched. I held my breath, feeling uncomfortably warm and queasy. She paused after seeing the impact of her words.

"I don't... I don't. I don't understand what you're saying to me. I'm a master's level student and I did well in your doctoral-level class. You're saying I don't belong," I said, fighting back tears. I would not allow this lady to see me cry, no matter how badly she tore me down.

Obich leaned forward, never broke her smile, and explained, "You're a hard worker. That's what you should be. That's your place."

If you were to transpose the features of a gremlin onto her real-life face, it would come close to the demonic image imprinted into my mind during this interaction.

I tried to make sense of our conversation as I walked back to my office. When I reached the reading room near my office, I ran inside, slammed the door behind me, and curled up in a fetal position on the floor, crying. For the first time in my life, an educator tried to keep me from getting an education.

My meeting with Professor Obich cracked the foundation of my belief system about my academic abilities, making me question my entire life. By fourteen years old, I knew I wanted to study linguistics and become a scholar, which would require obtaining a doctorate. My ninth grade English teacher, Ms. Aleen Jendian, suggested I apply for the Gates Millennium Scholarship. At eighteen years old, I was one of one thousand students to receive a ten-year award from the Bill & Melinda Gates Foundation. This achievement opened the doors to my lifelong dream and Professor Obich was the only roadblock standing between me and my goal. I felt so defeated, I threw away my only acceptance letter.

That same day, an email arrived from Professor Obich asking, "Did you ever decide what you want to do with your life, LaNysha?"

For a week after receiving Professor Obich's email, I didn't know how to respond. Her negative feedback filled me with self-doubt and she robbed me of my confidence. Instead of believing in myself, I accepted her idea that maybe a PhD was too out of reach for "people like me."

My mother's repeated advice echoed in my mind as I struggled to respond to Professor Obich: "Think before you act and speak. What you do and say is a reflection of where you come from, where you're going, and who you are. Know this." It took me two weeks to construct a seventy-two-word response.

This advice transformed my feeling of utter defeat into resolve. Professor Obich would not have the last word concerning my path toward my goal—that belonged only to me. After expressing surprise, I sarcastically thanked Professor Obich for her guidance. I then told her I had accepted a position as the national research director for a nonprofit and would teach as an adjunct professor until I finished my doctorate. I suggested she read Dr. Mark Taylor's *New York Times* op-ed about ending the university as we know it to "make higher learning more agile, adaptive, and imaginative."

Despite my initial reaction, once I internalized her criticism it took years for me to free myself from Professor Obich's discouraging words. Eventually, I proceeded to do what I wrote to her. Six years after our last encounter, I obtained my PhD.

STOP SURRENDERING YOUR POWER

Me Power is a book that teaches you how to tap into the limitless power that resides within, even when circumstances or other people present barriers outside of your control.

Before talking about what Me Power is, I must acknowledge the real and disempowering effects of limiting circumstances and oppression. Generally, disempowerment appears as apathy, lack of hope, and a lack of influence over one's own destiny. Studies have shown when disempowerment is present, individuals believe nothing can be done about a problem. They are convinced their actions will make no difference, so they give up.

My personal introduction to disempowerment began with Professor Obich. I became disempowered when I abandoned my autonomy and authenticity. I let her words keep me in a holding pattern, preventing me from taking the next steps toward achieving my dream. Two years after that meeting with Professor Obich, her words still haunted me. I accepted her belief I didn't belong in any doctoral program. Once I internalized her venomous words, my sense of self-worth was shattered and I started to impose limits on myself. I began making decisions based on her opinions rather than my own.

It is important to understand oppressive situations can create psychological conditions that give rise to debilitating emotions, which can last for a long time after the conditions themselves have changed (in my case, contact with Professor Obich). Internalizing oppression and discrimination is not victimhood, yet it can contribute to one occupying a victimized position. This position is temporary for some of us; for others, it is not.

I already had doubts because of my background. A single teenage mother raised me until she married when I was ten years old; my dad dropped out of high school; no one in my entire family had even completed college. Despite the fact that I worked while completing my degrees, I spent years believing and internalizing Professor Obich's words—that I was a worker bee unable to produce intellectual material.

Surrendering my future to her judgment made me feel powerless. To summarize:

- I internalized what she said and it became a barrier I could not even see, let alone embrace.
- My focus was off kilter. I wasted too much time and energy lamenting the fact that I wasn't good enough to get into a top-tier doctoral program, even when I was accepted into one.
- I muted aspects of who I was to bury my hurt feelings.
- I was unable to see a path to my goal and I had no guidance until I felt safe enough to share my story.
- I refused to think about my experience with Professor Obich but no matter how hard I tried, I couldn't forget it.

What I've learned since then is that we do not have to be victims of our circumstances. We are powerful beings and can cocreate worlds of our own design. I call this (Our) Me Power.

This book reveals how to use Me Power—the potent combination of self-knowledge and principled action—to catalyze change for yourself and/or the learners in your life. I want you to recognize you are capable of more than you think. You're already good at what you do—so good, in fact, that sometimes it's easy for others to take advantage of you or undervalue your work. But if you're willing to believe in yourself, even when others don't, there's no limit to what you can accomplish.

It's time to recognize your power within. Your inner strength is generative and the best of you will make an impact that reverberates in the world within and around you.

THE MISSING INGREDIENT IN EDUCATION: YOU

Before I met Professor Obich, I experienced school as an empowering context. I attended two elementary, three middle, and three high schools in Southern California because my stepfather was in the navy. I was fortunate enough to find teachers at these schools who nurtured my academic curiosity, inspired me to learn, and encouraged me to develop a strong sense of self. Most importantly, they created empowering conditions under which I knew my life was an autobiography in the making. In high school, I found myself empowered knowing that if I maintained a commitment to self-knowledge and principled action in an ever-changing (dialectical) social world, I could fulfill any dream. It was not until later I realized this feeling was Me Power.

Education is more than schooling. It's a dynamic process in any learning environment that shapes the way we think and interact with the world around us. Our introduction to education as an ecosystem is in school, where we're taught and socialized by our teachers, other educators, and peers. Schools exist to socialize children and educate them, creating an environment where students learn to conform to societal standards.

Social norms suggest you should be able to tell everyone where you're headed next, but this kind of collective knowledge doesn't come without consequences. It often misses teaching you how to learn, unlearn, and relearn who you are over time.

In high school, we are made to feel *who we are* is contingent on the answer to the question, "What is next in your life?"

The question of what to do in life continues into college, where students are often forced to choose a path before exploring their interests, having to answer: "What is your major?"

In the working world, this transforms into, "Where do you see yourself in five years?"

And as we age, the questions become more complex: "When do you plan on having children?"; "What does retirement look like for you?"

The expectation is that everyone can answer these questions with certainty and the answers will fit nicely into a timeline—an education followed by a career.

These questions boil down to a single inquiry, "How will you chart your course through life?" while ignoring the fundamental question, "Who *are* you?"

Choosing to *be* the answer is more important than finding it. Empowerment begins with the declaration, "I choose." To make this declaration, you must know yourself.

What do you remember when you think about the most empowering lesson in your life?

I'm guessing you're probably not thinking about information gained in a classroom.

Let's get one thing straight: the current education ecosystem of K-12, higher education, and workforce development does not prepare students to empower themselves. Whether we work as educators or have only been on the receiving end, we all know there is a serious problem with the state of education in the United States. The gap between what we learn in school and how that knowledge applies to life is so pervasive, it's now a cliché. Michael Hansen, CEO of Cengage Group, correctly asserts in a *Harvard Business Review* article, "There's a direct disconnect between education and employability in the US, where employers view universities and colleges as the gatekeepers of workforce talent, yet those same institutions aren't prioritizing job skills and career readiness. This not only hurts employers but also sets the average American worker up for failure before they've even begun their career."

The way we learn has dramatically changed in recent years, as the Internet provides us with an almost unlimited amount of information with the click of a button.

However, our educational ecosystem has not adapted to this new era. The insights generated through neuroscience about how we learn have yet to be applied to the industrial revolution-esque system of schooling.

The growing gap between the number of jobs in highly skilled fields and the number of workers equipped to fill them illustrates this point well. The US Bureau of Labor Statistics projects a deficit of nearly twenty million qualified workers by 2030, indicating the demand for skilled workers is much higher than the supply. The latest research from the Korn Ferry Institute explains the United States could miss out on $1.75 trillion in revenue due to labor shortages—approximately 6 percent of its entire economy. As technology advances and businesses become more globalized, the gap between what students learn and what they need to know to compete for good jobs widens. In addition, many schools struggle to provide students with the skills they need to succeed after graduation. Furthermore, over 60 percent of jobs require a degree beyond high school, according to Georgetown University's Center on Education and the Workforce.

It's time to rethink the current paradigm and create a new one that better serves us.

START WITH WHO YOU ARE, NOT WHAT OTHERS THINK

We must reimagine our education ecosystem so it empowers students to know themselves and take charge of their own futures with principled action. In today's world, the most important skill to teach children, young adults, students, workers—all of us—is how to take control of their own learning, whether we are in grade school, college, the penitentiary, or corporate training. We can't rely on others to teach us everything we need to know.

We must take charge of our own learning, continually developing self-knowledge throughout our lives. But most of us aren't taught what it means to know ourselves. As a result, we don't know how to start the process of discovering who we are, what we stand for, and what we're really capable of. Empowerment requires knowing who you are and adopting a state of mind in which you refuse to define yourself by others' unsolicited perceptions, judgments, and expectations.

How, then, do we expect anyone to learn who they are, what they stand for, and uncover what they're truly meant to do? How many would go on to more rewarding careers or even more schooling if they better understood themselves?

In a global economy powered by technology, we must acquire knowledge, competencies, and mindsets that prepare us to continually learn new skills throughout our lives for a future we cannot predict. The outdated notion that we must first pursue knowledge outside ourselves rather than within is wrong. The drive for disciplinary knowledge over self-knowledge is based on an obsolete learning model.

Knowledge of self is the most important knowledge and all other knowledge must revolve around it. The self is like a circle, whose center point is our core identity and whose radius is our external traits. Once we understand the circumference, center point, and radii, we can further expand our knowledge in whatever direction we choose.

Schools, colleges, and universities are the nexus of adolescent and young adult life. Despite spending over fourteen thousand hours in grade school, many of us never learn how to dig deep in an educational system that prioritizes moving quickly through subjects, checking off boxes, and acing tests over self-examination and skill development necessary for success. Many think teachers are the source of all disciplinary knowledge, when their role is best described as facilitators of the complex relationship between teaching and learning. More often than not, educational pathways are too cookie cutter and don't allow for the kind of personal growth and empowered learning many people need. Too many leave school feeling frustrated, disappointed, and unsure about what to do next. This can be a source of friction in the workplace and negatively impact one's sense of fulfillment in life.

You should be living your life on purpose, with purpose, in whatever way you decide. But how do you take charge and choose?

WHY I WROTE THIS BOOK
My desire to answer this question led me to write *Me Power*.

I am compelled to write about empowerment because we need a new way of thinking and acting that moves us beyond outdated power models. The old models keep us on autopilot, where we do what we were conditioned to do without question. We must stop thinking of power as something we can authorize, give away, or take from others. Instead, we need to start seeing it as energy—a flow of possibility that can be tapped into.

Me Power is a term I coined to describe the ability to realize and exude one's authentic self to live a happy, productive, and fulfilling life. When we tap into Me Power as a force of energy, we can use that energy to create change in our lives and the world around us. I describe Me Power by using research, anecdotes, and interviews with people who exemplify the concept.

I will teach you how Me Power is a function of perspective and choices and how it can be used as a spark to light the fire for personal, professional, and organizational development. Together, you and I will guide your manifesting energy in the direction of realizing your deepest hopes and dreams. This book is the result of twenty years spent working in education, combined with extensive investigations into how Me Power works and why some people wield it more effectively than others.

These insights led to the development of five guiding principles essential to manifesting Me Power. These principles provide a framework to understand the true meaning of empowerment, so you can design a self-development practice to not only benefit yourself but also the social world in which we all live and operate. I'm hopeful that no matter what your background or situation is, you'll find value in practicing these principles:

1. Embrace Your Barriers (**M**otivated **E**nergy)
2. Focus On Your Strengths (**My** **E**ducation)

3. Speak for Your Life (**M**yself **E**xpressed)
4. Choose Your Guide(s) (**M**astering **E**xcellence)
5. Ritualize Your Reflection (You Are **M**ore than **E**nough)

These principles are active in your own life, whether you are conscious of them or not. By identifying, understanding, and practicing with deliberation, you will harness Me Power in ways where you transform yourself and change the world around you.

WHY WE NEED A NEW DEFINITION OF "EMPOWER"

Empowerment is a central aspect of how we relate to each other, but it is rarely defined or properly understood. By shifting our thinking from empower to Me Power, we become the active agents that create the change we need and want in the world. Inherent in traditional definitions of the word *empower* is the idea someone else will "empower" us. But empowerment is not something we receive like a gift. It is something we do; it is a process in which we engage in. Me Power challenges the notion that we need to be empowered by others. Me Power must be constructed from within.

Let's stop talking about empowerment as something that can be given from the outside and instead as something all of us can do for ourselves, by taking ownership of our own lives and learning how to make things better for those around us. Empowerment refers to the power that comes from within, once we choose to control our own lives by believing we can achieve our deepest hopes and dreams. Therefore, I argue Me Power is what empowerment and lifelong learning are all about.

If you're like me, you've probably had so many moments in your life where you thought about doing something and then stopped because of a barrier. Maybe it's a matter of not having enough time to do what you want, or maybe it's more complicated—you don't know how to do it or maybe a human is blocking you. Barriers can hold us back from reaching our goals, but they can also motivate us to overcome challenges and enrich the experience of what it feels like to accomplish a goal. My experience with Professor Obich illustrates this perfectly.

The best personal and professional development processes help us learn to become better versions of ourselves and create optimal environments for us to fully come alive. We must define and manifest Me Power if we want to live empowered lives. If you are ready to take this journey or want to encourage someone else in their own quest, I invite you to join me.

HOW THIS BOOK WILL BENEFIT YOU

Me Power is about two questions: 1) What is true empowerment? 2) How do people manifest it? I offer a clear definition of Me Power as the answer and an approach to help people excavate aspects of themselves, foundational to their lifelong learning journeys, within or beyond school.

Me Power provides tools everyone can use. You will love *Me Power* if you are an educator focused on how to get students to find purpose, own their learning, and reach their full potential. Whether you are an educator, parent, student, or anyone grappling with the question, "Who do I want to be?" *Me Power* will help you discover your self-identity is not fixed or unchanging, but ever expanding as you move through life.

This book outlines a framework for unpacking this question at different life stages, with Me Power at the center of how you or the learners in your life answer it. I address "you" as someone who wants to get in touch with Me Power, but I also encourage you to consider how the lessons of this book apply to important learners in your life, including colleagues, students, or children.

The more you interact with *Me Power*, the more powerful it will become in your life. You can always come back to this book as a resource, consulting it when you encounter particular areas that require you to reactivate your Me Power. I encourage you to underline passages of this book that resonate with you, write down your thoughts in the margins, and use it as your own guide for living with Me Power at the center of everything you do.

Me Power is divided into two parts, corresponding to the two questions that open this section. The chapters build on one another, clarifying misconceptions about empowerment, illustrating how Me Power is manifested through the five principles (e.g., Embrace Your Barriers,

Focus On Your Strengths, Speak for Your Life, Choose Your Guide(s), Ritualize Your Reflection), and prompting further reflection on how you can put them into practice in your own life. Each chapter revolves around a central argument: The idea that others must empower us is a fallacy because we have the power to make changes in our lives. While designed to follow a logical sequence, you can read the five Me Power principles listed in Part II in any order. Each chapter in Part II ends with a section called "From Principle to Practice," where you will find exercises and reflective questions to help you apply what you've learned.

No one else is you. That is your power.

PART I

ME POWER FOUNDATIONS

CHAPTER 1

EMPOWERMENT IS MISUNDERSTOOD

S.T.O.P. = Start to Open Possibilities

—RICHIE NORTON

Have you ever thought about what *empowerment* means?

It's a popular term without a clear definition. Most of the time, we hear it used in conjunction with a particular social problem, such as women's empowerment, Black empowerment, economic empowerment, or employee empowerment. Without looking up each definition, we can assume they all relate to overcoming structural barriers, given the population's needing "to be" empowered somehow.

According to Merriam Webster, *empowerment* means:

1. the act or action of empowering someone or something; the granting of the power, right, or authority to perform various acts or duties

2. the state of being empowered to do something; the power, right, or authority to do something

These denotations—the literal or primary interpretations of the word—miss the mark of empowerment's true meaning.

As a lifelong word lover and trained linguist, to uncover the history of the word, I went to the best resource for the English language, the *Oxford English Dictionary* (OED). The OED has six hundred thousand words with present-day and historical meanings and pronunciations with more than 3.5 million entries, spanning over one thousand years. Unlike other dictionaries, the OED is remarkable because each entry contains selected quotations of the word in use at the time, which shows precisely how and when particular words were used, spelled, and pronounced. The OED revealed a different meaning for empowerment's root word: *empower.*

To understand its true meaning, I focused on the inverse of its prefix *-em:* me. The word's prefix stems from French, Old French, and Latin, meaning "in" or "into." In doing so, I realized empowerment is a personal process of pivoting one's perspective inward. Traditional definitions, however, assume external forces control the process. Those who invade our lives with physical power, positional authority, social status, or wealth often intimidate us. They can take the power we guard so carefully, stealing the very essence of who we are. None of these definitions reflect the outcomes we can achieve through empowerment. True empowerment requires recognizing we are our greatest assets and that it is possible for us to reach any of our deepest hopes and dreams by activating self-knowledge and principled action (i.e., Embrace Your Barriers, Focus On Your Strengths, Speak for Your Life, Choose Your Guide(s), Ritualize Your Reflection).

First used in 1849, the OED defines *empowerment* as "the action of empowering; the state of being empowered." Taking a closer look at its etymology, the transitive verb *empower* has been used in English since the seventeenth century, when Hamon L'Estrange (in *The Reign of King Charles*) and John Milton (in *Paradise Lost*) used it to indicate someone or something else enables power to emerge in unclear ways.

But what about the power that comes from within you, which you manifest when you become more of who you are, creating change and working to reach your maximum potential?

Sadly, my beloved OED disappointed. But the process of examining the word's use over time revealed a fact that was not at all obvious: Right down to its bones, empowerment is always a matter of power. In its popular use and etymology, empowerment has more to do with *power over,* referring to an externalizing effect of controlling, impacting, or influencing others. In fact, *power over* is the opposite of empowerment, yet the two terms share a similar meaning, both referring to giving someone else power or authority.

I cannot talk about *power* without mentioning the scholars who have been most influential in shaping my thinking on the matter, namely Michel Foucault, Hannah Arendt, Jo Rowlands, and Seth Kreisberg. These scholars have contributed to the school of thought which argues power is a relational force that can be used for positive or negative purposes. *Power with* is a kind of power between people who work together toward a common goal or vision through an organization, solidarity, and joint action. *Power to* means effective choice, the capability to decide actions, and carry them out. *Power over* is an oppressive force that distributes resources unequally and marginalizes those who are powerless; it is coercive, often violent, and all about hierarchy and domination.

In the *Oxford English Dictionary, power* is most commonly defined as one's ability to have his or her will carried out despite resistance from others—in other words, *power over*. This definition is probably why empowerment has an ironic meaning.

Three main ideas create a misunderstanding of what empowerment is truly about:

1. Distribution of Power Over;
2. The Wrong Locus of Control; and
3. Zero-Sum Game.

DISTRIBUTION OF POWER OVER

The first idea that contributes to a misunderstanding of empowerment relates to the distribution of *power over*. If empowerment is a process of being given the authority to change individually and within organizations, then who holds the power to allow such change to occur?

Our taken-for-granted meaning of the word presumes an external owner of power who gives power to others. We often think of empowerment as it relates to **others** rather than **ourselves**. As a result, we think only others can empower us before we are able to empower ourselves. Therefore, we need to take a closer look at the embedded meaning of *power over* and how that contributes to our misunderstanding of empowerment.

In statistics, a power law describes how two numbers are related. A change in one quantity results in a proportional relative change in another quantity. In other words, there's a cause-and-effect relationship between two things, where one gets bigger or smaller depending on what happens to the other.

The Pareto Principle, or the 80/20 rule, is a popular example of a power law distribution. It states that approximately 80 percent of consequences are from 20 percent of the causes. Let me underscore a fact behind this thinking: There is a limited amount of power that can be distributed.

For example, let's say you have a manager who has to distribute shifts among employees on a weekly schedule. The manager is in the authorizing position, so they set the schedule and then distribute it to you and your coworkers accordingly. The finite amount of time and number of employees working at any given moment means there are only so many desired shifts available each week. You and other workers will vie for the best shift because the schedule affects your lives. A change in one variable, such as too many people calling out sick on the same day, will result in a proportional relative change in the work schedule.

We often think of power as a scarce resource: Some people have more than others, so we assume they also are more powerful. But what if we thought of power as bound by a system, as opposed to being available in fixed amounts, waiting to be distributed? If each system has its own boundaries and rules, then there's an unlimited amount of power available to each person. Even though one person might be able to make more decisions than another, they're still limited by the bounds of the system itself—and so is everyone else. Managers can set schedules and give shifts, but they cannot determine what is best for their employees—that's for the employees to decide. Why? Because Me Power is owned by the individual, not the manager, who you might think has more "power." This might seem counterintuitive at first, since most employees feel like their managers have all the power. Many managers incorrectly think of empowerment as a distribution of power. The power that managers have over decisions gets distributed down to employees, who then become "empowered." But, from another perspective, managers are also limited by the bounds of their system (which includes their employees). They can't do everything themselves. The best companies create conditions for employees to flex their Me Power by providing them with the tools they need to solve problems on their own, without having to wait for approval or direction from management.

This is the approach that Best Buy's Twelpforce took.

From 2009 to 2013, Twelpforce used a team of more than three thousand Best Buy employees and Geek Squad agents to answer customers' questions via Twitter. Over four years, Twelpforce sent more than sixty-five thousand tweets with an average answer time of twelve minutes or less. John Bernier, one of the main creators of Twelpforce, used this practice to remove barriers for employees, by putting the tools in their hands to learn from one another and create a community of consumers who felt heard. As a result, Twelpforce helped improve the company's bottom line. Unlike traditional customer support services, employee access to Twelpforce was not restricted to a select group of highly trained agents.

By reducing *power over* distribution, Best Buy unleashed powerful knowledge already inside its employees. Giving up a traditional model of *power over* distribution made the company as a whole even more powerful, not less. In describing the company's distributed decision-making process, Gina Debogovich, director of social media, told the *Wall Street Journal*, "There is no right answer often." According to several case studies of Twelpforce's success featured in *Fast Company* and the *Harvard Business Review*, these efforts translated into more engaged employees, satisfied customers, and increased business for Best Buy. In 2022, for the seventh year in a row, Best Buy was named in *Fortune*'s list of the world's most admired companies.

Instead of thinking of power as a finite resource that can only be distributed from one person to another, what if we redefined it as something infinite and ever present, which everyone already embodies? What would it mean to live in a world where each person on the planet was empowered?

WRONG LOCUS OF CONTROL

After experiencing a rejuvenating weekend near Taos, New Mexico with friends at Ojo Caliente, a hot mineral spring resort in Northern New Mexico, I was revved up to take on the day. As an evaluation specialist for the Academic Literacy for All research project, funded $1.5 million by the US Department of Education, my task for the day was to complete six classrooms across three schools in two districts, then make it to campus for a doctoral seminar course in the evening. Armed with my second cup of Piñon coffee, this time with a shot of espresso, I took a deep breath, smiled, and walked into the classroom ten minutes early.

"Hi, welcome to seventh grade English. I'll have you sit at my desk in the back of the room," the teacher I was observing explained.

"Ms. Heather Bolles, my seventh grade English teacher, would be proud. I'm in seventh grade for a second time," I laughed as I took out my clipboard with the observation form.

"Wow! You still remember her?"

"I'll never forget Ms. Bolles. I was new at Castle Park Middle and she made me feel like school was my second home."

The students filed into the classroom and the teacher turned to greet them, quickly finishing the task of writing that evening's homework on the whiteboard. She took a roll call and all thirty students were present.

Her warm-up activity required students to write their names on a sheet of paper and pass it to the next person, so that each student had a sheet of paper not initially his or hers.

"Now that you have a sheet of paper with your classmate's name, please write one positive statement about them and pass it to the next person. We will keep doing this until you have the paper with your name again."

Highly engaged, the students seemed to like writing nice things about their classmates and passing the sheet of paper to others. Most of them remained silent without being told to do so, earnestly participating for eight minutes.

"In one word or phrase, how did doing this make you feel?"

A couple of students spoke up and answered "reflective" and "good."

I was taking notes on my sheet about the feel-good nature of this exercise and wondering what the focus of the teacher's lesson would be, given that she was setting up the learning environment in such a safe, affirming, and engaging way.

"One word to describe what you all did is empowerment. You all empowered each other with kind words."

The smile dropped from my face as I sat there raising a quizzical eyebrow.

"How can you use words to empower others?" she asked as the students paired up and then reported back.

After ten minutes, pairs of students shared examples about complimenting a stranger, thanking an acquaintance for her hard work, and telling someone she looked nice. After the initial warm-up exercise, the teacher transitioned into the main part of her lesson, asking students to select a topic, conduct research, and write an essay that would be due in a couple of weeks.

I forced myself to shake the confusion I had around the idea that students could empower each other with kind words.

"What does it mean to empower someone?" a student asked. You could tell by the tone of his voice he was confused.

The teacher smiled, having anticipated this question. She lifted the screen hiding the whiteboard, then read aloud: "Empower is a verb. To empower an individual or group means to help them become stronger, more successful, or more confident."

What I heard in the student's question, and what annoys me about this notion is the underlying idea that empowerment relies on someone else's approval. Kind words are nice, but the idea that we need someone else to say them to us to have agency and take action is problematic. It's crippling to think about what others may or may not think about us. We can believe in ourselves without depending on the approval of others.

Too many people focus on the wrong locus of control, thinking power exists outside of them rather than within them. Believing others should empower you reflects an external locus of control. Popularized in the 1960s by psychologist Julian Rotter, this social learning theory describes a continuum where we believe control lies in our lives—within ourselves or outside ourselves. When people have an internal locus of control, they believe their actions and decisions determine the outcomes in their life. Those with an external locus of control believe outcomes are determined by fate, luck, or others with power. When the locus of control is external, we believe good and bad things happen as a result of other people's actions and forces outside of our control. We think we have no power over what happens to us and therefore we can't do anything about it.

I've felt this way when other people's hurtful words or actions made me feel powerless. While the teacher I observed had kinder intentions, her lesson about others making students feel good is no less disempowering.

We need to believe we have the power and agency within ourselves to choose how we live our life, regardless of what others think or say about us. Why should we wait for the right words to give us the confidence needed to take action? The idea that we need someone else's approval to be empowered is detrimental to our growth because it implies power lies outside of us. It also reinforces the idea that we are not in control of our own lives. Regardless of what anyone else says or thinks about us, we can use Me Power to achieve our hopes and dreams. We empower ourselves, not other people or circumstances around us.

Where is the source of *your* power?

ZERO-SUM GAME

A zero-sum game describes a situation where for one person to win, the other must lose. Zero-sum thinking works like this: My success means your failure. If you're better at something than I am, then I must be worse. If you win a prize in a competition, then that means I have lost. If you get promoted at work, then that means I was passed over for the opportunity—and worse, I never had a chance to apply for it. This way of thinking pits people against each other in an "us" versus "them" mentality.

Zero-sum game and the distribution of *power over* are two different concepts, but they have a lot in common. Both are characterized by the belief someone either gains or loses. These two types of thinking overlap when we apply power-over thinking to zero-sum situations, by focusing on who won or lost instead of looking for opportunities for everyone involved.

Many people think of empowerment as a zero-sum game based on the false idea that we can empower people by taking power away from others. A zero-sum misunderstanding of empowerment says we must give rights or privileges to one group at the expense of another group—if one group wins, then another loses. According to this mindset, if women gain rights and privileges, men suffer; if LBGTQIA+ people gain rights and privileges, straight people suffer; if people of color gain rights and privileges, white people suffer; if people living in poverty gain rights and privileges, wealthy people suffer, and so on.

This misunderstanding fails to realize that empowerment means elevating yourself first, then others. At its core, empowerment is about sharing knowledge and resources with one another so everyone has a chance to succeed in their own right. For far too long we have subscribed to the idea that empowerment is a zero-sum game, where one's gain comes at the expense of another's. This way of thinking has permeated our society, so much so that the language we use reinforces it.

American segregated pools illustrate how much zero-sum thinking costs us as a people. In *The Sum of Us*, Heather McGhee explores how towns all over the United States shut down their swimming pools as a protest against integration. The shutdown of these swimming pools is an example of zero-sum thinking. It's also a depressing metaphor for the way racist Americans abandoned public investment both in their communities and in themselves. McGhee's most vivid example was in Montgomery,

Alabama at Oak Park in the 1950s, an idyllic space with a large swimming pool, wading pool, pool house, and tennis courts. Surrounded by flower beds, walkways, and a granite pavilion, Oak Park even had a tiny zoo near a pond. But it was a whites-only space.

Before black people could even use the space, McGhee explains, "They drained the pool, filled it with dirt, and closed Oak Park. They sold off the animals in the zoo, shut down the entire parks and recreation department of the city, and kept it closed for a decade. [It wasn't until 1970] the good people of Montgomery even got to enjoy a public park again, all because of racism."

We need to completely reject this way of thinking and we can do so by understanding two key points:

1. People who are different from you (in race, class, gender, sexual orientation, or anything else) being empowered does not take away your own power; and
2. Empowerment is not finite, but infinite.

When it comes down to it, a zero-sum worldview fundamentally opposes the idea of empowerment.

What we need is a movement that believes empowerment is an unlimited resource and turns us into a united front for change—in other words, (Our) Me Power.

Me Power is empowerment. No one will ever give you power; you have to claim its abundance for yourself. The first step? Tap into (Our) Me Power.

(OUR) ME POWER ACTIVATION

- Empowerment is not what we think it is. Because the use of the word *empower* is ubiquitous, we do not question its meaning.
- How do you define empowerment?
- Misunderstanding the true meaning of *empower* has profound effects on how we view empowerment in our lives and how we think about ourselves as individuals and contributors to society. We naturally assume there is an external owner of power who can give it to us if they wanted to—the person who's in charge of hiring decisions at work, for example, or the manager setting our work schedule, or the person who runs our school system.
- In thirty seconds, list all the words you can think of associated with empowerment's base word: *power*. How many of the words on your list have to do with control and domination?

CHAPTER 2

(OUR) ME POWER DEFINED

Unless we understand our lives as a kind of autobiography in the making, we're likely to take refuge in other people's stories, in ready-made ideologies, and in unexamined systems of belief.

— SCOTT LONDON

The danger of individuals taking action without critical thought has never been more exemplified than by the horrific crimes committed by Hitler and the Nazis during World War II. The Nuremberg trials, a series of thirteen trials held between 1945 and 1949, charged the top surviving German leaders with crimes against peace, war crimes, crimes against humanity, and conspiracy to commit any of these. (Bamford, 2020)

What was the defense?

Obedience.

At the Nuremberg trials, the first international war crimes tribunal in history, Rudolf Höss, the longest-serving commandant at Auschwitz concentration camp, explained, "We were all so trained to obey orders without even thinking that the thought of disobeying an order would simply never have occurred."

The Nuremberg judges rejected this defense. They asserted a person has a choice whether to follow an order, even if that person does not know the order itself is illegal. The "following orders" defense as justification for murder on a heretofore unimagined scale exposed the depth of legal and moral corruption that permeated the Nazi regime. The court's findings led to the Genocide Convention, which defined genocide as a crime that can take place both in times of war as well as in times of peace. The United Nations accepted the Genocide Convention as its first human rights treaty and most countries in the world agreed to follow it.

Lack of self-knowledge + inhumane, unprincipled action = crime against humanity

Stanley Milgram, in his now-famous obedience experiments at Yale University in the 1960s, set out to investigate key questions that emerged from the Nuremberg trials: Were these Nazis unique in their obedience because of a single charismatic leader? How easily can ordinary people be influenced by a recognized authority to commit acts they might hesitate or object to carrying out based on their moral or legal understanding?

Participants were falsely told the study investigated the effects of punishment on memory and learning. Milgram organized his research study around three roles: The first role was the experimenter, who stood and provided instructions. The experimenter held the ultimate authority position, providing the structure and setting the norms of how the research participants were to behave. The second role was the actor, aware of the purpose of the study and never actually shocked, but designated as the "learner," sitting in an electric chair. The third role was the "teacher," a voluntary research participant, sitting in front of an electric shock generator with thirty switches ranging from 15 volts (slight shock) to 450 volts (danger to severe shock). The teachers were told to administer an electric shock every time the learner made a mistake, turning the dial to increase the voltage each time.

Out of forty, how many "teachers" do you think dialed up the shocks to the highest level, prepared to inflict fatal voltages on their students?

Almost two-thirds of the "teachers," or sixty-five percent, pressed every single one of the thirty switches on the electric shock generator.

Despite its many ethical and methodological problems, Milgram's experiment indicates most people obeying commands feel less responsible for their actions because they do not take ownership over things that are within their control. Over the past sixty years, others have replicated the experiment many times in several countries, all with roughly the same results. Three factors contributing to this kind of "thinking" are:

1. There's an authority outside of us that exerts power, to whom we are subordinate.
2. We are powerless to change external forces and surrendering is best for our wellbeing.
3. Your "power" can only be obtained at the expense of someone else's power. Therefore, when we possess it, we must protect it no matter the cost.

Milgram warns, "The most fundamental lesson of our study is that ordinary people simply doing their jobs, and without any particular hostility on their part, can become agents in a terribly destructive process. Moreover, even when the destructive effects of their work become patently clear, and they are asked to carry out actions incompatible with fundamental standards of morality, relatively few people have the resources to resist authority."

Me Power aims to equip readers with the resources they need to stop yielding their power to a real or perceived more powerful other.

THE TRUE MEANING OF EMPOWERMENT
Now that we've seen the dark side of traditional conceptions of empowerment, it's time for us to redefine the word.

As I've mentioned before, to get to the true meaning of empowerment, I focused on the inverse of its prefix -em: me. Grammatically, me is a pronoun and functions as the objective case of I. In other words, the main difference between the two pronouns is that I is a subject pronoun and me is an object pronoun.

As you will see, me is not only a first-singular object pronoun; it can also serve as an acronym. I emphasize me first to remind us of the importance of our uniqueness and the need for self-knowledge and principled action, as we navigate relationships with others. You might remember from middle school a subject pronoun can replace the noun—person, place, or thing—performing the action—verb—in any sentence. For example, I electrically shocked my students. An object pronoun, on the other hand, may replace a sentence's direct object, indirect object, or the object of the preposition. The object pronoun receives the action of the verb or shows the result of the action. It's not "me ran" but "my students ran to me." The object pronoun, me, receives the action of the running students.

While drier than unbuttered cornbread, these linguistic details are important because my combination of "Me Power" is grammatically incorrect. I'm calling out these technicalities because I took what on the surface looks like a prefix, -em, flipped it into a personal pronoun, me, and created "(Our) Me Power": a concept that is a noun, not an overused verb implicating people as passive recipients.

Me represents the first person singular so the individual starts with himself or herself. Yet, Me Power doesn't stop at the individual and is not a silo based on some narcissistic conceptualization of inner power.

Unlike empowerment's denotative meaning, I argue *power* in Me Power refers to power within based on one's knowledge of self, manifested as a result of you becoming more of YOU, taking principled action, and working with others to reach your maximum potential. Me Power is the opposite of unthinking obedience.

$$Knowledge\ of\ Self + Principled\ Action = Me\ Power$$

THE ME POWER FRAMEWORK

To explicate Me Power as a concept, I explored several combinations of ideas. After two years of unpacking the concepts through direct and secondary research and interviews, I noticed a pattern of five components: Motivated Energy, My Education, Myself Expressed, Mastering Excellence, and More than Enough. Each "ME" represents one of five interrelated parts of ourselves.

You can develop each of these components through an associated guiding principle and practice: 1) Embrace Your Barriers, 2) Focus On Your Strengths, 3) Speak for Your Life, 4) Choose Your Guides(s), and 5) Ritualize Your Reflection(s). Together, these Me Power principles and practices provide a framework for people to understand the true meaning of empowerment; in turn, this understanding helps design a self-development practice to benefit individuals, first, and then the social world in which we all live and operate. How you apply the five principles facilitates your expression of Me Power. The Me Power Framework, shown in Figure 1, helps provide a structure to the messy process of learning that is required as we become more empowered.

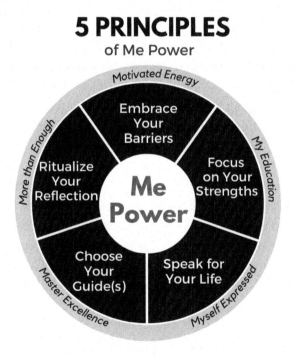

Figure 1: The Me Power Framework

While covered in Part 2 in more depth, the five principles of Me Power focus on aspects of our humanity that emphasize actions we take to become empowered. The associated principle explains the process/outcome and the acronym describes the how-to and vice versa. For example:

1. Embracing Your Barriers is key to how you use **M**otivated **E**nergy to excel.
2. Focusing On Your Strengths is the foundation of **M**y **E**ducation, within or beyond school.
3. Speaking for Your life is how you express yourself (**M**yself **E**xpressed) and the multiple versions of self you create throughout your lifespan.
4. Choosing Your Guide(s) is essential as you **M**aster **E**xcellence.
5. Ritualizing Your Reflection helps you remember you have and will always be **M**ore than **E**nough as long as you are your own standard.

The manifestation of (Our) Me Power, by definition, is a social process since it occurs in relationships with others. The individual and his or her community are fundamentally connected. Me Power is a journey, one that develops as we work through it together. Yet for each aspect of Me Power, individuals define what ME means and looks like for them.

(OUR) ME POWER = WE-NESS

(Our) Me Power is a play on words meant to get us thinking about the power we each have within ourselves and how we choose to use that power to improve our lives and uplift one another.

(Our) Me Power is the very thing that distinguishes us from primates. Michael Tomasello (2018) builds on Jane Goodall's research, whose groundbreaking work in 1960 disproved the notion that tools were uniquely human since chimpanzees make and use them, too. Tomasello's research reflects more than three decades of work aiming to answer, "How do humans differ from other great apes in cognition and sociality?" On the *Social Science Bites* podcast, he says:

> *"We-ness" that can mark human behavior is replaced by the "me-ness" of other primates. Humans put their heads together, as a general phrase, to accomplish things that neither one can do on his or her own. So if you look at all the things you think are most amazing about humans—we're building skyscrapers, we have social institutions like governments, we have linguistic symbols, we have math symbols, we have all these things—not one of them is the product of a single mind. These are things that were invented collaboratively at the moment or else over time as individuals build on one another's accomplishments.*

Shared intentionality, as shown through social cognition, social interaction, and language, is what makes us human and explains our sense of "we-ness" over "me-ness." We-ness, or shared intentionality, refers to how people see themselves as belonging to a larger whole whose members work together for mutual benefit. Social cognition is the ability to learn from, cooperate, and communicate with others. While unique across cultures, the fact that all humans create social norms and for the most part, live by them, is built into our DNA.

For example, Tomasello and a team of researchers tested how a pair of three year olds split items up. In the experiment, the researchers had the children work together but gave one more items than the other. The "lucky" child then gave some extra to his friend, which researchers found happened nearly 80 percent of the time. For a control condition, researchers had the children work alone, without any prompting, and gave more items to one child than the other. The "lucky" child still gave half of their share to the other child nearly 40 percent of the time. These results, which have been replicated many times, show children have very strong ideas about fairness, even when adults aren't around to give instructions.

Tomasello's research demonstrates humans cooperate in ways that are unique to our species. Science proves that chimps are not like humans, despite sharing 98.8 percent of their DNA. When Tomasello and his team conducted the same experiment with chimpanzees, they got completely different results. If a chimpanzee received one treat by himself, he was just as likely to keep it all to himself whether he received it through teamwork or not. Collaboration and fairness did not matter to chimps.

The heart of (Our) Me Power has to do with interdependence more than independence. My assertion is supported by what Tomasello and researchers call the Interdependence Hypothesis, which posits that "at some point, humans created lifeways in which collaborating with others was necessary for survival and procreation." Interdependent collaboration is essential to understanding the way empowerment, as defined as Me Power, operates. Based on evidence from our evolution as a species, if people work together, they can do more than they could do alone.

THE WE INSIDE OF ME

On December 10, 1996, a blood vessel erupted on the left side of Dr. Jill Bolte Taylor's thirty-seven-year-old brain. It all started with a throbbing headache that would not go away. When she started to lose her balance and could not stand up straight, she explained her epiphany in "My Stroke of Insight," her TED Talk with over twenty-eight million views. It's also the second most viewed TED Talk of all time. Dr. Taylor recounts realizing, "'Oh my gosh! I'm having a stroke! I'm having a stroke!' The next thing my brain says to me is, 'Wow! This is so cool! How many brain scientists have the opportunity to study their own brain from the inside out?'"

As a trained neuroanatomist and an expert in the scientific study of the nervous system, Dr. Taylor worked at Harvard University as a brain scientist. A colleague alerted first responders and rushed her to the hospital after hearing her speak gibberish on the phone due to a stroke. Miraculously, Dr. Taylor survived after experiencing a stroke for several hours. Two weeks later, the doctors "removed a blood clot the size of a golf ball that was pushing on [her] language centers." Ultimately, it took her eight years to recover, with the help of her mother, friends, and chosen family.

Dr. Taylor's TED Talk highlighted the peace she found once she chose to thrive in the right hemisphere of her brain, which controls attention, memory, processing of visual shapes and patterns, emotions, and problem solving. Even though both the left and right hemispheres communicate with each other, because they process information differently, their experience is completely different. Dr. Taylor described a disconnectedness that is characteristic of the left hemisphere: "As soon as my left hemisphere says to me 'I am,' I become separate. I become a single solid individual, separate from the energy flow around me and separate from you. And this was the portion of my brain that I lost on the morning of the stroke."

Dr. Taylor described the interconnectedness she experienced when she lost the ability to speak, read, walk, write, or remember because of the golf-ball-sized blood clot in her brain. When people think of a stroke, they usually think of all the things you might forget. But sometimes when you have a stroke, it can make you connect to things in unexpected ways. Now Dr. Taylor has more connections than ever before. She exemplifies (Our) Me Power because of her poetic description of the interconnectedness, where other people are part of her and she is part of them—what Dr. Taylor describes as "the 'we' inside of me." She questions:

> *So who are we? We are the life-force power of the universe, with manual dexterity and two cognitive minds. And we have the power to choose, moment by moment, who and how we want to be in the world. Right here, right now, I can step into the consciousness of my right*

hemisphere, where we are. I am the life-force power of the universe. I am the life-force power of the fifty trillion beautiful molecular geniuses that make up my form, at one with all that is. Or, I can choose to step into the consciousness of my left hemisphere, where I become a single individual, a solid. Separate from the flow, separate from you. I am Dr. Jill Bolte Taylor: intellectual, neuroanatomist. These are the "we" inside of me. Which would you choose? Which do you choose?

In no way is Me Power meant to be interpreted as an obsessive interest in one's own power *over* other people. That would be antithetical to the conceptualization of (Our) Me Power described above. As an acronym and first-person singular object pronoun, *me* serves as a reminder to ground ourselves in our uniqueness as we navigate relationships with others in the social world. Me Power is self-knowledge and principled action, coupled with owning one's inner power, positively expressed in communion with others. Me Power comes from knowing yourself and being true to yourself when in a group. Self-awareness, self-love, and accountability are hallmarks of Me Power. Me Power is flexed by activity.

THE ME-NESS OF IT ALL
Me. Me. Me.

Some people may argue Me Power promotes self-absorption and self-obsessiveness. Based on the use of the first-person singular object pronoun *me* alone, Me Power could be perceived as a homage to the Me Decade, Me Generation, and the Me Me Me Generation that followed. A *Time* magazine article explains, "In the US, millennials are the children of baby boomers, who are also known as the Me Generation, who then produced the Me Me Me Generation."

In the 1970s, the young Baby Boomers, most of whom were young adults, wanted to find out who they were. According to psychologist Jean Twenge, a leading researcher examining generational differences, Baby Boomers are the most well defined of the twentieth-century generations, named after the post-World War II birthrate spike that began in 1946. Many young Boomers in the 1970s examined who they were by listening to their bodies and trying different things previous generations never would, such as hallucinogens, like LSD, public workshops where people shared intimate details about their lives, getting naked in public, or streaking, and engaging in shameless sexual revolutions. Perhaps this is why in the August 1976 issue of *New York Magazine*, Tom Wolfe wrote a long piece defining the seventies as the "Me Decade," which he characterizes as "changing one's personality—remaking, remodeling, elevating, and polishing one's very *self* [...] and observing, studying, and doting on it. (Me!)"

If we go with Wolfe's characterization, self-indulgence and having an excessive interest in oneself—in other words, narcissism—is the defining feature of any me-centric foci. Unfortunately, narcissism appears to be on the rise. According to Twenge's and her colleague's most popular study, a cross-temporal meta-analysis of eighty-five samples of US college students over a twenty-four-year period, found that between 1982 and 2006, narcissism increased by 30 percent. They examined the responses of 16,475 college students nationwide who completed an evaluation called the Narcissistic Personality Inventory (NPI), a tool commonly used by psychologists to identify both clinical and borderline narcissism. At the end of the study, Twenge and her colleagues point to *Time* magazine's declaration of "you" as the Person of the Year in 2006 as indicative of the increase in narcissistic people. Of particular interest is their statement, "The rise in narcissism may have influenced the ways people use technology [because so much of our current technology] permits self-promotion far beyond that allowed by traditional media."

In an article in *The Guardian*, organizational psychologist and *New York Times*-best-selling author Dr. Tasha Eurich explains because we live in an "increasingly 'me' focused society," most people find it easier to "choose self-delusion over the cold hard truth."

In her book, *Insight: The Power of Self-Awareness in a Self-Deluded World*, Eurich expands on this concept by explaining we have a current "cult of self," which promotes a "widespread, low-grade narcissism." This is evidenced by our technological focus—what she calls "Selfie Syndrome"—and the growing "me" focus throughout society at large. She warns, "An intense self-focus not only obscures our vision of those around us; it distorts our ability to see ourselves for what we really are."

While an overt me-centric focus may raise concerns about narcissism, it is the focus on the self that ironically diminishes self-knowledge. In contrast, Me Power is not *just* me focused. It is what I call me first in its focus. Me Power describes the self-empowering attitude you must have to succeed. If you've activated Me Power, you're willing to look in the mirror, see the good and bad, and accept it all as a part of who you are. You're willing to change what needs to be changed and accept yourself for who you are, flaws and all. Being true to yourself means accepting who you are at any given point in time, being proud of that person, and knowing you have the strength to change if that's what you choose.

To do so, I encourage folks to adopt the following perspective: I'm a human being. I exist in the world, and the world exists around me. Me Power is about what it feels like to live in the world and to experience the fact I'm alive. People experience a sense of Me Power because of their ability to transcend their individual circumstances and experience themselves as part of an interconnected whole, or what Dr. Taylor calls "the 'we' inside of 'me.'"

Self-absorption happens when a person is too wrapped up in their own lives to a fault, while a me-first philosophy is being aware of your unique circumstances and doing what's best for you in relation to others.

WHAT ME POWER ISN'T

Most of us have heard the preflight announcement, "In case of a cabin pressure emergency, put on your own mask first before assisting others."

On a flight to Boston from DC with my first son when he was five months old, I was surprised when the flight attendant tapped my shoulder and emphasized I needed to put on my mask first before I could even think about putting one on the baby. It seemed counterintuitive. Why would I not help my baby first?

I am sure I've heard that message hundreds of times. But this was the first time I sat on the plane and really thought about what it meant, partially because I spent nearly twenty-two hours in labor with my son, Davidson, and I couldn't fathom not rushing to put his mask on first in a plane crash.

"If a plane crashes," I said to myself aloud, "you need oxygen to live. To get more oxygen, you first put on your own mask. Once you have a mask on, you can help Davidson with his mask."

I looked down at my baby boy, with his perfect blonde curls and almond-shaped blue eyes. We locked eyes. He smiled and cooed, while I panicked knowing I would not abide by these airline safety guidelines. I knew conceptually our survival depended on me taking care of myself first, yet part of my brain would not accept that I had to wait to assist my baby.

Then I remembered a YouTube video I saw explaining the science of this very well-established air travel safety rule.

In the video, Destin Sandlin, an engineer who created the *SmarterEveryDay* Youtube channel with over ten million followers, enters a special chamber with an astronaut to find out what happens if you don't put on your mask first. After three minutes and forty-five seconds, Sandlin starts to lose brain function and cannot identify basic shapes. Soon, he can't even speak or put his mask on and someone must step in and put it on for him to prevent him from dying.

As cabin pressure drops in a plane, oxygen levels also drop and hypoxia becomes a real concern. The effects of hypoxia, a deficiency of oxygen reaching the brain, become greater the longer you go without oxygen. Astronauts and aviators have to undergo hypoxia training so they know when their brain is about to stop working correctly and when they must take immediate action. Sandlin emphasized that at thirty-five thousand feet, you only have seconds of useful consciousness: "You can go from a normally rational person to someone so helpless, you can't even save yourself if your life depends on it."

Between the exhaustion of new motherhood and the thought of potentially having to sacrifice my infant son, a light bulb went off.

If I run out of oxygen, then I literally cannot help save Davidson.

Self-absorption can be defined as the philosophy of me, first and only, whereas a self-first perspective is always in relationship to others.

Me Power is about putting your mask on first, meta-phorically. Yet, you cannot express Me Power without some sense of "we" or community.

(OUR) ME POWER ACTIVATION

- What does Me Power mean to you?
- Where do you feel you could put Me Power into action in your life today?

CHAPTER 3

THE POWER OF
KNOWING WHO YOU ARE

*The paradox of self-knowledge is that it's only
by confronting the depths of our own ignorance
that we can begin to glimpse the essential truth
of who we are. Knowing, as the mystics have
always said, begins with not knowing.*

— SCOTT LONDON

Information isn't knowledge.

Google, launched in 1998 and responsible for 92 percent
of all searches on the Internet, makes it easy to explore
any topic. We have a whole world of information at our
fingertips, satisfying answers to our questions at any
given moment. On average, Google processes over forty
thousand search queries every second, which translates
to over 3.5 billion searches per day and 1.2 trillion searches
per year worldwide. Google's function is so ubiquitous
it has achieved verb status. In this digital age, we have
access to so much information that it's easy to think we

know everything, or at least enough about everything. When there is so much to know, you can often mistake thinking about something as knowing something. But even if you have an opinion on every topic under the sun, there's a good chance you don't actually know as much as you think you do.

Research in neuroscience has demonstrated the human brain is wired to believe it knows more than it actually does. Our brains have evolved to help us make quick decisions, but because of this, it can be tempting to draw conclusions about things without actually knowing the facts. This happens all the time. The more we hear something, the more likely it is our brain will accept it as true. This is why people have opinions on topics they don't actually understand—they've heard someone else's opinion enough times their brain accepts it as truth without any critical thought. Our Google world makes this problem even more severe, as our searches bring up a mix of facts and opinions masquerading as facts.

This needn't be sinister. Take, for example, a popular belief that fish only have a three-second memory span and every lap of their fishbowl is like seeing the world for the first time. We've seen this perpetuated in the Disney films *Finding Nemo* and *Finding Dory*, where Dory, voiced by Ellen DeGeneres, suffers from short-term memory loss and cannot even remember her name. In 2008, Rory Stokes, a teenager from Adelaide, Australia, put the three-second myth to the test when he conducted an experiment with his pet goldfish.

He took a red Lego block and put it in his fish tank whenever he fed the fish, sprinkling the food around the block. Three weeks into the experiment, the fish had learned to associate the Lego with food and would swim toward it looking for sustenance. In those weeks, the time it took the fish to reach the Lego decreased from over a minute to just under five seconds. Then, for six days, Rory fed the fish without using the red Lego. When no food was offered and the red Lego was reintroduced, the fish still knew finding the red Lego meant food was eventually on its way, thereby proving their memory is much longer than three seconds.

A year after Rory's experiments, scientists at Technion – Israeli Institute of Technology in Haifa taught young fish to associate a certain sound with feeding time. They then released the fish into the wild, and five months later when the fish were adults, researchers played the same sound. Surprisingly, the fish swam back. Other researchers have found fish can tell time by being conditioned to push a lever at the same time every day and can even be taught how to drive using a small vehicle! Rory and the research scientists pushed beyond popular information about fishy memories to pursue knowledge on their own terms.

IT'S NOT LOST, IT'S FOUND: KNOWLEDGE OF SELF

We all have a tendency to overestimate our knowledge and underestimate our ignorance. There's even a name for this phenomenon—the Dunning-Kruger effect. It's named after two researchers who found people who are unskilled at something tend not to recognize their lack of skill. In fact, they often believe they're above average in their ability. Yet, if we are skilled at something, we may *underestimate* our abilities. This flawed self-assessment is one of the significant blind spots standing in our way.

Our brains and minds try to adapt the information around us to confirm our assumptions and beliefs. To understand how we can overcome our biases, it is necessary to look at what causes these blind spots in the first place. The Dunning-Kruger effect reveals itself in the tendency to assess our own skills and abilities in comparison with those of others. We must be aware of two common cognitive biases, which may interfere with how we understand who we are, including 1) confirmation bias: we interpret others' behaviors in ways that reaffirm our preconceived notions about them, and 2) illusory superiority: when comparing ourselves with others, we tend to overestimate how much better off we are than others on most dimensions of comparison.

For a long time, information we accessed to make decisions was filtered only through what we could gather from our immediate surroundings. Today, however, there is an ever-increasing amount of accessible information. It's a double-edged sword. On one hand, it means we're capable of learning more than ever before, but on the other hand, it means people are far less inclined to trust their own judgment and are more likely to look toward outside sources for answers. When we have access to so much information at the click of a button, it's difficult not to question our own instincts and take things at face value. It's easy to fall victim to the Dunning-Kruger effect when we limit ourselves in this way, especially when we talk about who we are.

The *self* becomes an object of study when we apply it to who we are. When we speak of *self*, we use the object pronoun *me* to refer to it, reflecting the linguistic foundation of Me Power covered in Chapter 2. Human beings are in a perpetual process of becoming, by definition. To be truly self-aware, we need to go beyond a basic definition of *self* and understand it as something separate from our identity. James Clear points out *identity*, based on its Latin roots, literally means "repeated beingness," explaining why habits are more about *who* you are rather than what you do.

Our identities are more than just our experiences and our personalities. In other words, our repeated histories form the aspects of who we are. The information we use from our past provides a snapshot in ways that aren't necessarily knowing—and that's okay. After all, how could we possibly expect anyone to know everything? What's important is how we use what we do know to learn more about the things we don't. The more we open ourselves up and engage with others, the more we can grow from each other and exchange ideas. That's the only way to bridge the gap between thinking you know something and actually knowing.

This is why learning is so important: It allows us to expand our understanding beyond the boundaries of our immediate surroundings and explore new ideas and opinions with an open mind. If you want to really understand and know, you need to challenge your own beliefs, starting with an examination of who you are.

When we try to make sense of the big picture of life, what is important and what is not, how our choices in each moment will affect us later on, how people will react to our actions, and so on, we often rely on the information that comes from our own experiences. When we have this experiential information, it's easy to assume we are in a position where we can make decisions with confidence. It's only when a situation forces us to face something we are completely ignorant of that we recognize how little we actually know. If you don't know how much you don't know, you will be unaware that your lack of knowledge makes it difficult for you to recognize situations where your expertise isn't enough. If this is the case, it follows the most effective way to become aware of what you don't know is to consciously examine what you do know.

More than ever before, the keys to success are tied to your ability to learn on your own from anywhere. Thirty years ago, UNESCO's International Commission on Education for the Twenty-First Century sought to answer a key question: "What kind of education is needed for what kind of society of tomorrow?" UNESCO is a specialized agency of the United Nations, aimed at promoting world peace and security through international cooperation in education, arts, sciences, and culture. In 352 pages, UNESCO's report proposed an integrated vision of education based on lifelong learning and the four pillars of learning—to know, to do, to be, and to live together. Viewing learning as a knowledge of self-journey "throughout life enables us to view education in all its dimensions, both as a tool for individual and social advancement and as an end in itself."

Formal education, the report asserted, tends to emphasize certain types of knowledge to the detriment of others, proving it is essential to sustaining human development: "Education is not just institutionalized education. There is a dynamic at work between 'schooling' and the educational alternatives, a dynamic based on complementarity, but also a process of change, a questioning of the practices and the partitions of knowledge."

In sum, we need to put *self* at the center of all attainment of knowledge.

Although we don't typically think of education in these terms, self-knowledge contributes to lifelong learning. Through a practice of learning, unlearning, and relearning who you are, you can begin building a stronger foundation for manifesting Me Power and becoming the best version of you.

Everyone else is already taken.

A NEW LEARNING CYCLE WITH "SELF" AT THE CENTER

When it comes to knowledge of self, it's helpful to think about it as a learning triad cycle of unlearning, learning, and relearning. Unlearning refers to the process of letting go of old ideas, beliefs, and behaviors that no longer serve you. Learning refers to the process of acquiring new ideas, beliefs, and behaviors that can better serve you. Relearning refers to the process of returning to old ideas, beliefs, or behaviors that once served you, but have been lost along the way.

We live in a world of constant change and flux. When I was younger, I was taught there were nine planets. Now, there are only eight planets because Pluto was classified as a dwarf planet. A normal planet has enough gravity to be the center of its own orbit, while a dwarf planet is smaller in size and revolves around the sun with other planets. In today's rapidly evolving, information-rich environment, it's essential to learn new information and skills and adapt quickly.

The highest forms of learning are unlearning and relearning. Unlearning is about releasing yourself from the past and being open to new things and ideas. It's about letting go of what has been and embracing what is yet to be. In contrast, relearning is about reengaging with an old skill or concept in a new way or applying the wisdom gained from past experiences to what we know now. We're constantly learning, unlearning, and relearning throughout our lifetime.

Before embarking on the learn-unlearn-relearn learning cycle, you must commit to minimizing blind spots by identifying what you think you know, confronting it, learning new things in areas where you think you've mastered something, and seeking feedback from others. Eurich's (2017) work emphasizes the fact that we all have blind spots. We believe we know what's going on in a given situation, but we often fail to see the things right in front of us. This is especially true when it comes to how we present ourselves to others, whether it's at work or in our relationships.

Our self-perception is subject to cognitive bias and even our own evaluations are often inaccurate. We're all blind to certain aspects of ourselves. As humans, we are subject to our own biases and shortcomings. Because we cannot always assess what we know, how we feel, or how we behave, we have work to do to overcome these blind spots. This makes it important to ask for guidance from selected others, covered in Chapter 7.

While we should not make decisions based solely on our own opinions, we also should not rely too heavily on others' opinions. Relying too much on others' opinions while operating from a lack of self-knowledge can be dangerous. Let's take the case of Cheryl Rich, who, after becoming pregnant at age eleven, developed a drug addiction and served time for a criminal conviction. Afterward, she became a clinical psychologist and the executive producer of Fox Soul's *The House*, helping others transform trauma and fears into a life of joy and fulfillment. We'll keep coming back to Cheryl's story throughout this chapter.

Unlearning is necessary because it gives us a fresh perspective on the things we thought we already knew. It allows us to start chipping away at the layers of social conditioning that have been laid down over our lifetime.

It's about breaking down the walls between us and the world around us so we can reconnect with ourselves and with each other. It's about getting rid of all those self-limiting beliefs that hold us back from doing what we love because they were never true in the first place. It's about stripping away all the fears we gathered along the way and replacing them with courage and confidence.

Cheryl spent a lifetime unlearning the labels others put on her:

> *You could imagine how fragmented and fractured my entire being—the inner core of my being—was after such an experience. So I did not find the words or the understanding that I am as unique as my finger-print. I shouldn't have to pay for anyone to love me. I shouldn't be seeking approval. Yes, I'm a human being. And human beings want connection and we want to be loved. But until I approve of me, I will not get the energy back. So coming through drugs, jails, and hell, literally, from a little kid pregnant at eleven and the addiction to self-torture taught from a mother who was living in self-torture. I came from that through heroin use, a prison stay, a child who I simply hated and could not mother, could not nurture, and into such self-loathing that I wanted to die and attempted suicide a few times. It took me many years to climb out of the pit of self-hatred hell.*

Unlearning means freeing yourself from limiting beliefs and ideas about who you are, what you're capable of, and how things work in this world. This is a core essence of Me Power. Me Power is the combination of self-knowledge and principled action. It means being able to see things clearly without preconceived notions or judgments getting in the way.

Unlearning is like wiping away smudges off your glasses so you can see things more clearly. If you've ever felt like there's a fog hanging over your head, preventing you from seeing things clearly, that's probably because there is! Others may have taught you certain things about yourself and the world at large that keep you stuck in certain thought and behavior patterns. These ideas become entrenched in your thinking and influence who you think you are.

In Cheryl's story, the external labels of "preteen mother," "drug addict," and "convicted felon" interfered with her ability to see herself. She eventually realized, however:

> I already got what I got in me that no one else has and other people will eventually see it. Because now I have owned my God-given power. Me Power/empowerment is when you decide that you are enough. It's when you realize that you are who you are, as unique as your fingerprint. You can start to study "me." Your birthright of peace of mind is when you understand you have Me Power. By becoming aware that you really are taught to live inside of chaos and confusion, and catch that "I'm not enough disease." It's a disease in the mind, which creates dis-ease in the body.

EMBARK ON LEARNING-UNLEARNING-RELEARNING JOURNEYS

Applying the unlearning, learning, and relearning processes to self-knowledge means knowing who you are and embracing all of it—including the parts of yourself you might not like or society may judge you for—and figuring out what fits with the rest of your life to create an integrated self.

What if you could see yourself as you truly are? What if you had a mirror that showed you not only your reflection but also your innermost being?

This is the art of self-knowledge, an inward-facing journey that allows you to see who you are now and who you will choose to be in years to come. But in broader American culture, most do not prioritize this kind of self-knowledge. We're often taught to seek external sources of validation—to compare ourselves with others and ask, "Am I good enough yet?" This approach only leads to disappointment, or worse, makes us feel like we will never be good enough.

As we see in Cheryl's story, the turning point came when she went to prison: "I had to find a way to finally look in the mirror without seeing the monster looking back at me. My reflection was still that monster, but the monster—suddenly I could see it. My own reflection was a monster. And I had tracks running up and down my arms from shooting drugs." It was in prison, "having everything stripped away, I couldn't go use any drugs. I had no place to hide. And the journey started."

To live empowered lives, we must see and know ourselves.

Through self-knowledge, we can learn about ourselves without comparing ourselves to others or trying to measure up against some arbitrary standard for what makes us acceptable human beings. Self-knowledge is about taking responsibility for our thoughts and actions, not just in terms of what happens outside of us, in the world, but also inside of us, in our minds. It's about taking stock of our thoughts, beliefs, emotions, habits, and behaviors, then asking, "What do these things *about* me mean *for* me?"

The ancient Greeks devoted philosophy and literature to the pursuit of finding oneself. The Temple of Apollo (Delphi) is located on the southwestern slopes of Mount Parnassus above an impressive amphitheater tucked into the natural crescent formed by the mountains. Located one hundred miles northwest of Athens, ancient Greeks considered the temple sacred as the gods bestowed divine prophecies upon select mortals, most notably the Oracle of Delphi. The temple walls bore this simple yet powerful message: "Know thyself."

What does it mean for you to know *your* self?

In the Me Power framework, knowing yourself is based on three dimensions related to universal needs we all have as humans. These are: 1) personal well-being, 2) connection with others, and 3) making a positive difference in the world. In *The New IQ*, Dr. David Gruder argues these three dimensions are core drives based on authenticity, connection, and impact. These three dimensions are what human development is all about, so much so that we have a three-dimensional self—one dimension for personal authenticity, one for relationships, and one for serving the larger collective we all belong to. Thus, one's self is active, dynamic, malleable, and embedded in the social world.

Why embark on this journey of learning, unlearning, and relearning our "self?"

No kind of knowledge is more important than self-knowledge. It allows us to sort through various flows of information bombarding us every day. Knowledge of self means knowing what you want, why you want it, and how committed you are to getting it. It means knowing what you're passionate about and what drives your passions. Self-knowledge isn't just about knowing yourself; it's also about knowing others because we are all products of our environments and our interactions with others.

In their groundbreaking work *Deep Learning: Engage the World Change the World*, Michael Fullan, Joanne Quinn, and Joanne McEachen explain, "What gives humans meaning in life is a strong sense of identity around a purpose or passion, *creativity and mastery* in relation to a valued pursuit, and *connectedness* with the world and others." Learning about others can help us learn about ourselves. This kind of learning doesn't only happen in school. If we pay enough attention, we can see it happens everywhere.

It is not an overstatement to say the world is in a state of chaos. It's hard to know what to believe, who to trust, and how to live. With so much going on in the world, it's easy to get caught up in the day-to-day buzz of our lives and lose sight of what matters. What is important? How can we make sense of this madness? The answer, as always, is education.

Knowing ourselves builds a foundation upon which we can discover the meaning and significance of disciplinary knowledge, which we can learn in engaging ways. Disciplinary knowledge refers to the in-depth content knowledge of a certain type of curriculum or subject. Our own identities provide the most relevant, possible approach to understanding disciplinary knowledge, which helps us to develop skills, abilities, and the habits of mind we need to learn.

EDUCATION IS MORE THAN SCHOOLING

For many people, education is about the information you learn and not knowing who you are. The focus on consuming information in pursuit of a credential or degree is not enough. Knowledge requires understanding, which includes unpacking the reasons behind our opinions and beliefs in a way that contrasts them with other opinions and beliefs. When we move away from self-knowledge, we risk defaulting to cognitive biases, which make us believe we know more than we do or pay selective attention to things that confirm our beliefs while ignoring those that contradict them.

Because education is about so much more than what you know, we need to start teaching knowledge of self is foundational to every aspect of learning. This idea, in and of itself, requires unlearning because the current educational system centers on a transmission model from the nineteenth century. We assume if we can just get enough information into the head of every student, they will be successful, productive citizens.

The transmission model of learning focuses on disciplinary knowledge first and self-knowledge second—and we wonder why students are not engaged or empowered! When this happens, students don't understand disciplinary knowledge, don't care about it, and don't apply it to their lives. The transmission model assumes there is a neutral body of knowledge that exists outside the student and teacher, which can be transmitted from the latter to the former. But as we know from our lived experiences, this is not true. All disciplinary knowledge is situated in history; therefore any claim to it is already laden with sociocultural power dynamics.

For students to understand themselves better, they must engage with their own histories and contexts; they need to recognize how they are situated within larger social structures and how those structures affect their lives. We need to teach them how to critically analyze these structures— how they interact with others and how they relate what they're learning back to themselves. But this cannot happen through traditional pedagogical methods because these methods assume students have an objective understanding of reality—an understanding that can be transmitted from one person, the teacher, to another, the student.

The study of economics in schools illustrates what it would look like to start with self-knowledge and then layer in disciplinary knowledge. Economics is the study of how people make decisions and allocate resources, so it's a perfect example of a discipline that starts with self-knowledge. When students are asked to examine the social and cultural contexts that shape their economic world, they are forced to think about who they are in relation to their economic system. This kind of self-knowledge helps students see how their identity impacts the way they live, which can help them understand how systems around them impact their lives. In fact, many economics classes run a simulation in which students virtually participate in the stock market without trading real money. Students that win typically use self-knowledge as the foundation for improving their understanding of the stock market and financial literacy.

To flip this transmission model on its head, we need to prioritize self-knowledge over disciplinary knowledge. We can take the best pedagogical practices of what we already know and put it through a new filter, known as relearning, so we can reprioritize the knowledge we most value. We pick up new skills, release old practices, and adapt to change all the time. As a result of our ability to adapt, we undergo constant learning, unlearning, and relearning—remaking ourselves in the process.

In Cheryl's case, relearning first required letting go of the labels and dependency on self-torture. She then learned a new way to "control the judgment, the voices inside [her] mind," and relearned how she would engage in body-based experiences, moving from unhealthy to more healthy practices:

When I decided to consistently commit to taking time out for myself, my body, my mind, I began understanding the power of breath being long, slow, and deep. Without the breath, all the rest doesn't even matter. Now, I can find the silence between the chatter inside my mind, of the voices inside of my mind, of judgment. Taking that long, slow, and deep breath helps quiet the mind, because the mind can't think of two things at one time. My practice is walking on a beach, marching in place, rolling around on the floor like a kid, doing yoga, and swimming every day. These [actions] gave me seconds of silence between the judgment in my mind that rewired my brain.

THE LAYERS OF WHO WE ARE

The older we get, the more we become set in our ways. We form habits and patterns that make us feel safe and secure. It's easy to get too comfortable, believing we have reached a point where who we are is static and unchanging. But this couldn't be further from the truth. Who we are is never static. It's constantly changing and evolving, as we gain experiences and learn more things.

When we fail to challenge our own assumptions about identity, we limit our potential, threatening our ability to manifest Me Power. But by unlearning our assumptions about who we are, we can discover new ways of looking at the world, which leads to greater understanding and increased self-awareness.

If you're already a self-aware individual, this might be old news for you. But for many people, as soon as they get past the basics of who they are—their gender, their age, where they live, what they do for work—they stop questioning themselves. They even stop questioning the ideas that have been passed down to them from their friends, family, and society at large.

Cheryl Rich is a prime example of what it means to reveal oneself over the course of a lifetime, questioning in the most powerful ways to unlearn-learn-relearn her *self.* She's survived the unthinkable: becoming a mother at eleven years old, a "felon" by twenty-five, and burying her only child when she was thirty. With a bachelor's degree from Kent State University, a master's degree in clinical psychology from Antioch University, and certifications as an intervention specialist and a victims assistant mediator, Cheryl seeks, attracts, and unearths solutions for those in desperate situations. Explaining where she is now at sixty-two years old, she says:

> Now I'm in the mindset of everything is as it's meant to be. I can go to my breath long, slow and deep. Access my power. Find the silence between the chatter of judgment, bam, I got my birthright: peace of mind. Staying in the mindset of being in the moment from where my view is the one thing that will, of course, make me aware. I've got the

power. I've got Me Power. I am empowered. I don't have
to live my life in fear and addicted to chaos and confusion
and making excuses for people who don't treat me fairly.

Throughout the duration of our lives, we all go through the process of discovering and rediscovering who we are and what our life's purpose is. Who you are is not just a collection of past experiences and recent changes, but also an accumulation of everything you've ever gone through in your lifetime. You do not become who you are from one single event. You're the product of your past, present, and future selves. The past self is where we believe we can find answers to our problems. The present self is where we live and breathe. And the future self is where we hope to go. The point is, who we are today is not necessarily who we'll be tomorrow.

The most important factor in education is not what you know, but who you are. Your identity is like a tapestry, woven together from the threads of your life. You chose some of those threads and some were chosen for you. Each thread represents a moment or experience in your past, which may stand out on its own. When put together, the threads create a whole greater than the sum of its parts. You wouldn't be who you are without them.

It's hard for us to see ourselves as just one person, because it feels like we're in three places at once: a past self who made mistakes, a present self trying to fix those mistakes, and a future self who will reap the benefits of those fixes. It's not easy to harmoniously integrate our experiences. But these three selves aren't different people—they're different parts of ourselves that coexist. We always live in all three places at once—it's just our perception that separates them into distinct categories. Each time we make a decision, we create a new version of ourselves—one that has never existed before and will never exist again.

When we ask high school students or college graduates what they want to be, or interviewees where they see themselves in five years, we force them to think about the future in terms of a question that doesn't necessarily have a clear-cut answer. The expectation that you should be able to tell everyone where you're headed next often leads us to disregard the process of learning, unlearning, and relearning who we are over time. Knowing ourselves is the center, a foundation upon which we can build an understanding of disciplinary knowledge to learn in ways that engage us most and allow us to find the greatest meaning. When we know ourselves, Me Power is ours to manifest. The learning triad—a cycle of unlearning, relearning, and learning—is an ongoing process, essential to cultivating principled action in this world.

UNDERSTANDING YOUR "SELF"

It's easy to get caught up in everyday stressors, family obligations, and work responsibilities without taking the time to learn about yourself. Even though most people *believe* they are self-aware, Eurich and her team found only 10 to 15 percent of the people studied fit the criteria required for self-awareness. Eurich outlines seven specific categories of self-knowledge that self-aware people continuously develop, what she calls the "Seven Pillars of Insight," including:

1. **Values:** The principles that guide us
2. **Passions:** What we love to do
3. **Aspirations:** What we want to experience
4. **Fit:** The environment we require to be happy, energized, and engaged
5. **Patterns:** Our consistent ways of thinking, feeling, and behaving
6. **Reactions:** The thoughts, feelings, and behaviors that reveal our strengths and weaknesses
7. **Impact:** The effect we have on others and the world around us

The self-knowledge process of learning, unlearning, and relearning can help you learn more about the tapestry of who you are and how your essence unfolds over time. This process relies on learning, unlearning, and relearning to make sense of who we are in the world. In today's fast-paced world, we can't assume someone will teach us everything we need to know as we go along. In fact, people are more likely than ever to stumble upon new ideas and experiences without having a teacher at the ready to help them understand.

Your self today is not the same self as it will be tomorrow. Who we are is not based solely on the family and place we were born into. *You* choose who you become, not your personality, your parents, or anything fixed. Our environment and the people we surround ourselves with, two things we take for granted, deeply influence our choices. However, they are not the determining factor: *you* are.

Executing this process involves pursuing two significant types of self-knowledge: internal and external self-awareness. Self-awareness is a complicated concept, but it boils down to the ability to see ourselves clearly—to understand who we are and how others see us.

Internal self-awareness refers to understanding ourselves from an inward perspective. It refers to the ability to understand and interpret our own actions, thoughts, and feelings. It allows us to gain insight into our true motivations, values, and feelings, rather than being influenced by the opinions of others or by what we want other people to think about us.

External self-awareness refers to understanding ourselves from an outward perspective. It's the awareness other people have of us and how they perceive us. It's influenced by an interaction between our public image—what we project to others—and their own experiences with us. The external view of ourselves empowers us in social situations because it gives us the ability to handle feedback constructively and objectively.

Self-knowledge is a journey, not a destination. It's not about getting to a certain point and then being done with it. It's about being in the moment, exploring your strengths and capabilities, and taking steps forward every day. The self is like an onion. When you peel one layer, you find another. The more layers you uncover, the more you realize how much work there is to do. You peel back layer after layer, opening the onion to see what's inside. You peel off one layer and then there's another one underneath it, and you keep peeling away until you get to the core of your authentic self. No matter how much progress you make, there's always more to learn. This is Me Power in action and you will continue to hone it for the rest of your life as long as you choose.

(OUR) ME POWER ACTIVATION

- There is no Me Power without self-knowledge. Self-knowledge is the foundation of every aspect of learning and it's inherently social. Learning to unlearn, learn, and learn again is the basis of self-knowledge. Answer the question: how will I choose to learn, unlearn, and relearn something today?
- The first step in the learn-unlearn-relearn process is to figure out what exactly we think we know. Take a notebook or a voice recorder with you wherever you go, and as new information comes up, jot it down or talk about it into your microphone. Think about what you already know about that subject and then commit to identifying your blind spots—areas you may have a certain amount of knowledge in but still don't really understand.
- Write down three adjectives that come to mind when someone else mentions your name. What are the words they use to describe you? Ask five people who know you well to describe you using three adjectives and compare them to your original list. How do these words make you feel? Do these feelings match the way you see yourself?

PART II

ME POWER PRINCIPLES

CHAPTER 4

EMBRACE YOUR BARRIERS (MOTIVATED ENERGY)

Where there is no obstacle there is no way.

—DR. GEORGE C. FRASER

The previous three chapters of this book describe taken-for-granted beliefs about empowerment. I argue for a more precise definition, where we think of the verb *empower* as Me Power. It was necessary for us to first work our way through the nuts and bolts of the word's meaning. Now it is time to move forward to illustrations of Me Power manifestations.

Now that we've got a handle on what Me Power is, let's talk about its five guiding principles. You can think of guiding principles as guidelines that drive behavior or mindset when executing operational plans in life. The five guiding principles of Me Power provide universal and enduring guidance, applicable in all circumstances, regardless of changes in goals, strategies, type of work, or phase of life.

The first principle of Me Power is to Embrace Your Barriers. Barriers are temporary obstacles conquered only when we accept them as opportunities to learn and grow. The embrace is a choice you make to rethink what you experience and to welcome the uncomfortable feelings that accompany cognitive dissonance. Cognitive dissonance happens when you consider these barriers, which slow you down or attempt to stop you, are potentially for your own good. Once you psych yourself into action, you understand there is power in the choice to face obstacles head on instead of allowing them to overwhelm you. This Me Power principle emphasizes the importance of seeing obstacles as preparation for the unexpected—seeing them as opportunities and taking advantage of them by choice, even though you may not have had any choice in the barriers you encounter. You look at what holds you back and continue to move forward anyway. You don't have to have it all figured out—you just have to keep going.

During the pandemic, I joined the ParentPreneur Foundation, a nonprofit that provides community, resources, and capital to Black entrepreneurs who are also parents. This was a crucial step in practicing what I preach. I struggled to see how I could sustain my coaching and consulting company, Edlinguist Solutions, with a newborn and a two year old. I was without childcare while my husband was deployed. When I joined the community created by James Oliver Jr., he immediately connected me with other educators and provided grant money at a crucial time in my business. He also personally checks in on me to ensure I am emotionally solid. It is impossible for me to overstate how much this organization has meant to my life and the lives of my family members.

So, although barriers appeared, doorways opened that continue to foster the growth of dreams, the business, and the well-being of my children.

Well-known individuals who have met with members of the ParentPreneur Foundation in intimate virtual settings include: Seth Godin, marketing guru and author of twenty best-selling books in thirty-seven languages, Gina Bianchini, founder and CEO of the multimillion-dollar company Mighty Networks, and Dr. George C. Fraser, chairman and CEO of FraserNet, who President Obama awarded the President's Lifetime Achievement Award. In the fall of 2020, Dr. Fraser spoke of the importance of networking and the uniqueness Black culture equips us with, reminding us not to ignore the pathway to how we define success. He explains, "I eat failure and obstacles as vitamins. I actually love them both. I have failed fast and I have failed my way to success. And [with] every failure, every stumble, the first question I ask myself is, 'What did I learn?' The second question is, 'How can I apply it?' The third is, 'How can I use it for personal motivation?'"

Dr. Fraser shared his favorite quote outside the Bible by Marcus Aurelius: "The impediment to action advances the action; what stands in the way becomes the way."

Although this was not my first time hearing it, that quote struck a different chord in me because it aptly describes the first principle of Me Power. Dr. Fraser eloquently reminded us that every day we are faced with challenges and opportunities that can either propel us forward or hold us back from reaching our full potential. We must make sure we recognize these opportunities for growth so we can be prepared for them when they come knocking at our door!

By embracing your barriers, you will come to appreciate something about yourself that is unique in encountering those barriers. This self-knowledge and insight will reveal nothing can hold you back from taking action to accomplish your hopes and dreams. When you embrace your barriers, you don't just get through them. You also get something else: self-appreciation, or what Dr. Kristin Neff (2022) describes as the flip side of self-compassion. Once we embrace these barriers, we can move forward.

Embracing your barriers is not only a key principle of Me Power based on stoic philosophy but also grounded in many years of research. Turning this into a measure of resilience and researching it, Dr. Paul Stoltz calls the first principle of Me Power the Adversity Quotient (AQ). He defines AQ as the ability of an individual to think, manage, direct, and endure challenges and difficulties in life. AQ is based on four C.O.R.E. dimensions: Control (who is at fault here and who is accountable), Ownership (who has control over the situation), Reach (your ability to react), and Endurance (how long you're willing to stick it out). The AQ research base consists of over fifteen hundred studies from more than one hundred universities and organizations around the world. One's expression of Me Power and success depend on how well an individual can persevere in times of adversity.

A significant amount of research shows if you repeat something enough times, it becomes automatic. Unfortunately, many people don't pay attention to their thought patterns, so they don't disrupt habitual patterns to make changes. They just keep repeating the same thoughts and actions. To solve this problem, Dr. Stoltz has developed and tested a technique called the "LEAD Sequence." To increase AQ, you must:

- **L**isten to your response to adversity,
- **E**stablish accountability,
- **A**nalyze the evidence, and
- **D**ecide what to do about it.

In a world obsessed with succeeding in the absence of any limitation, it's easy to forget life is an ongoing battle against problems and obstacles. In reality, these things give purpose to our drive and direction to our passion. They help us set goals, strategize, and push ourselves further than we ever could without them.

MOTIVATED ENERGY (ME) POWER

The *me* component associated with Embrace Your Barriers is Motivated Energy. When you embrace your barriers, you accept them as part of the process and you turn these obstacles into opportunities to motivate your energy to excel.

It's also important to remember while you may face specific challenges today, this is actually good news because it means you're moving toward something worthwhile. It would be bad news if no challenge or barrier stood in your way—because then you'd be going nowhere. So when things get complicated, and the way forward seems impossible to see, take a moment to revel in your motivation rather than feel angry about your limitations. Motivated Energy doesn't just help you achieve more; it helps you find greater meaning in all you've accomplished along the way too.

Motivated Energy is a proven, effective strategy for helping people overcome obstacles and achieve success. Motivated Energy is based on several decades of research into human psychology and behavior, particularly as it relates to goals, habits, willpower, and decision making. On his blog and in his bestseller *Atomic Habits*, James Clear talks about motivation in terms of routine. Instead of looking for motivation or inspiration; he asserts you just need to start your routine. He describes the three Rs of habit formation: 1) reminder, 2) routine, and 3) reward. The action you take to get started on a difficult task and the habits you form to continue working is what Motivated Energy is all about. Motivated Energy comes from your desire and belief in something rooted in yourself and connected to something greater than yourself. Action drives motivation more than motivation drives action.

Maintaining motivation is absolutely crucial for achieving your goals. To maintain motivation over time, you must be aware of all the factors that create or limit your motivation levels. The clearer you are about what motivates you, what demotivates you, and how each plays out in your specific environment, the more effectively you will be able to use Motivated Energy as a tool to achieve success.

Embrace your barriers and you'll be unstoppable!

During my undergraduate years, I worked three jobs at all times. One of my favorite gigs was as a writing consultant in the writing center at Cal State San Marcos (CSUSM), where twenty of us served approximately eight thousand students each year. When students came into the writing center for help, a student-hired receptionist greeted them and directed them to sign in and have a seat until their appointment time arrived.

As a writing consultant, I offered undergraduate students feedback and suggestions on papers in progress. We met in one-on-one thirty-minute sessions for twenty to thirty hours a week. Popular with a few nontraditional students, including Juliet Cody, I became a trusted advisor. To facilitate conversations, I co-constructed a blueprint with students for how they would best approach their challenging writing tasks.

"Even though there's Braille in the elevators to help me navigate the campus, I always take the stairs," Juliet Cody explained.

Walking out of the writing center, located in the library's basement, I accompanied Juliet and her guide dog, Marly, to the bottom of the stairs leading to the Chávez Plaza. Students at CSUSM are well known as the Cal State Stair Masters for all the steps they choose to take. At CSUSM, every day is leg day.

Juliet and I stood at the bottom of the stairs, looking up as the sun shone on our faces. "There are 271 steps. Are you ready?" With a runner's rhythm, she galloped up each step as I struggled to keep up with her and Marly. At the top, a statue of César Chávez greeted us, with his famous maxim in bronze lettering: "*Sí se puede,*" or "it can be done."

"When I stop to talk to people, the smell of coffee from the cart straight ahead keeps me on track. I turn left, walk down the next flight of forty steps, and head to the first floor of the science hall for my classes on Mondays and Wednesdays."

Juliet also explained Marly remembered the routes for the many trips around campus—so much so that Juliet would give Marly a command for a location and she'd take Juliet there. Once we arrived at the science hall, I said goodbye to Juliet and Marly, then trekked to Markstein Hall for a technical communications class I was taking in the College of Business Administration.

I learned quite a bit about how excellent Juliet could navigate CSUSM, which required her to go up and down 250 steps multiple times a day. Additionally, Juliet's experience as a nontraditional student starting her higher education journey in her forties inspired me. While running a successful daycare center, Juliet was diagnosed with retinitis pigmentosa, a rare genetic disorder causing retinal degeneration. Instead of viewing her degenerative eyesight as a barrier that would prevent her from obtaining her degree, she shifted her mindset to embrace it head on. Juliet immediately learned Braille and began immersing herself in the community to stay active as she lost her eyesight.

You can't control what happens in life, but you do have the power to choose how you react.

What struck me about Juliet was her commitment to serving others, even though she had to learn a new way of living in and moving through the world. Her stance was one of choice where she learned to body surf, obtained an advanced degree in communications, and advocated for civil rights for the disabled. Inspired by the National Federation of the Blind, the largest membership organization for the blind in the United States, Juliet came to believe her blindness was a strength, helping her teach others about how to live independent lives and motivate blind people who may not believe such a life is possible. Juliet became a state board member for the National Federation of the Blind, forming three chapters and serving as president, served as a board member of CSUSM's Disabilities Issues Advisory Committee, and became president of the San Diego chapter of Guide Dogs for the Blind.

Obstacles accentuate what you are capable of—but that capability may not have an opportunity to rise to the surface until obstacles are encountered. Juliet's story exemplifies the first principle of Me Power, Embrace Your Barriers, in such a powerful way. While she had a good life before she lost her eyesight, she was not dedicated to a larger mission where the betterment of herself would benefit an entire community of people.

For her work in the blind community, Juliet received a national scholarship from Recording for the Blind & Dyslexic, a nonprofit organization that produces textbooks for visually impaired and dyslexic students. This highly selective and prestigious scholarship provided her an opportunity to travel to Washington, DC, meet privately with First Lady Laura Bush to discuss Braille literacy and issues concerning the blind, and influence legislation for the blind. By approaching barriers as opportunities to further grow, Juliet was able to come into her own and showcase her Me Power.

You can still exercise your power when the odds are stacked against you.

YOU HAVE A SECRET WEAPON IN YOUR DNA

Encoded in our DNA is the need to set goals and seek to accomplish them. Engaging us in ways that activate learning and psychological needs of fulfillment, getting from point A to point B is full of struggle. Take any goal as an example.

The minute we take a step to turn our dreams into reality, a number of internal and external obstacles will appear, almost out of nowhere. The emotions that arise in the form of fear, anxiety, and self-doubt are enough to discourage action beyond thought. The uncertainty of *how* and *when* these dreams will become reality presents us with so many unknowns, which can feel overwhelming for many.

That feeling of overwhelm can be debilitating when roadblocks keep recurring. If it's not one thing, it's another, right? If we can't be unyielding in our decision to forge forward, then the emotions associated with those ongoing roadblocks and obstacles will cause us to lose hope and traction.

A key first step to make your dreams tangible is to set intentions with goals, articulated both verbally and in writing. Tapping into our genetic predisposition requires us to turn on a crucial part of our brain, called the Reticular Activating System (RAS), when it comes to taking goal-setting actions (Levitin, 2014). In the human body, RAS sits at the base of the brain above our spinal cord, about two inches long and as wide as a pencil. It serves as the "attention center" of the brain, where all our senses come in, except for smell, and connects the subconscious part of our brain with the conscious part.

Have you ever been at a crowded event, so concentrated on the performance happening on the stage, that the once-loud bullhorns, chants, and voices of people talking become a kind of background noise? Then, out of nowhere, someone five rows behind you says your name and you hear it instantly, no matter how loud the crowd. That is your Reticular Activating System, or RAS, filtering the eleven million bits of information your human brain processes every second. In short, the RAS takes what you focus on, creates a filter for it, and seeks information that validates your beliefs.

Visualizations and affirmations work in the same way. In an interview with reporter Ed Bradley on *60 Minutes*, critically acclaimed Black American actor, director, and producer Denzel Washington shared when he dropped out of college for a semester with a 1.7 GPA and struggled as an actor, he visited his mother at the beauty salon she owned in New York City. On March 27, 1975, one of his mother's customers saw his reflection in the mirror and was moved to profess, "Boy, you are going to travel the world and speak to millions of people." The woman, who Washington did not know, then wrote, "This boy will speak to millions" on a piece of paper and gave it to him. More than forty-five years later, he still carries that paper and reads it often. To date, Washington has earned various awards including, but not limited to, two Academy Awards, three Golden Globe Awards, a Screen Actors Guild Award, and a Tony Award. In 2020, the *New York Times* ranked him as the greatest actor of the twenty-first century.

Activating RAS is the first step in achieving our goals. Yet, the latest research on the science of goal-setting proves that as powerful as our brain is, it cannot distinguish between reality and imagined reality. So, when we give ourselves a picture of the goal we want to achieve, the mind starts believing it is real. Arguably, Washington affirmed his prophecy as truth, allowing his subconscious mind to take over and act in accordance with that belief. RAS is an "attentional filter" that automatically shifts our conscious awareness and attention to only what is important—whether or not we actually define its importance. Setting a goal works, in part, because we set our RAS to pay attention to the things that will help us achieve the goal.

Even the act of writing your goals down stimulates RAS. When you physically write something down, the RAS focuses more closely on processing what you write. This, in turn, increases your ability to remember what was written and affirm what will be in the future has already come to be. Understanding RAS and its function, particularly with setting goals, helps to filter key information that can help you bring your intention to life.

Despite using RAS to accomplish our goals, we cannot avoid barriers in life. Achieving our deepest hopes and dreams requires overcoming obstacles. The path to success is never easy. Obstacles are inevitable—we can't avoid them—but we can choose how we respond to them. The key to turning roadblocks into opportunities lies within each of us.

BE A NO LIMIT SOLDIER IN YOUR QUEST

Take Percy Miller, more popularly known as Master P, for example. Master P created No Limit Records and an entire business empire, including a sports agency, ahead of what Jay-Z has done with Tidal, what Dr. Dre has done with Beats Electronics, and what Kanye West has done with clothing and art. In 1998, No Limit Enterprises grossed more than $160 million in revenue, a feat no other rapper had accomplished with a business.

The barriers Master P encountered over time showcase his strengths.

Growing up in a two-bedroom house with fifteen people in the Calliope Projects motivated him to pursue college, with aspirations to be an NBA star and provide a better life for his family. Living in an environment with so many people helped him realize his passions and talents early. His love for learning kept him in the library instead of the popular places in his environment. Calliope was one of the most violent housing projects in the United States based on murder and drug-related incidents. He made his first goal escaping Calliope and living past nineteen years old: "A lot of my friends were dying young and I wanted to live to be over nineteen. I thought I was gonna die before I met nineteen because all my friends were getting killed."

Master P earned a basketball scholarship to the University of Houston, but a terrible knee injury during his freshman year forced him to consider something different. He left Houston for Oakland, California, where he took classes at Merritt College, focusing on business. After a work-related accident resulted in the death of his grandfather, Master P inherited a ten-thousand-dollar malpractice insurance settlement check.

Combining his knowledge from books with his passion for music and entrepreneurial spirit, Master P opened a record store in Richmond and mainly catered to the Bay Area, selling rap music featuring local artists such as Tupac, Too Short, and E-40. The store quickly became a hit and Master P started selling his own music at the store, under his newly launched No Limit Records label. By networking, he could circulate his music to DJs and connect with the artists he uplifted, opening for Tupac and Too Short. With the success of his first two albums and the record store, Master P moved back to New Orleans to be with his family and turn his attention to building the No Limit label.

No matter the barrier or uncertainty ahead of him, Master P held fast to the vision and belief that he would accomplish his goals. From his example, we see a certainty that cannot be shaken—that he would manifest his vision. He's resolute, with an understanding his actions would lead to a successful outcome—eventually.

Impressed by his success as an independent artist, Jimmy Iovine, cofounder of Interscope Records and later Beats Electronics with Dr. Dre, approached Master P with an offer to sell the No Limit label. He built an amazing company that had attracted an opportunity of a lifetime: one million dollars. Living in the projects at the time, Master P desperately needed the money. This offer to sell was a blessing. During this part of his life, Master P faced many financial struggles as it was difficult to obtain a loan, which would help offset some of the expenses of running his music label. Master P, however, turned down Iovine's offer.

In a recent podcast with host Dee Brown, *The Sky's the Limit*, Master P implored, "You have to know your worth." On the one hand, he references monetary value, but on the other hand, he taps into the root of one's self-worth and belief in something money cannot buy. After taking a closer look at Iovine's offer, Master P used his knowledge of business and understanding of contracts to know he would have had to sign away the rights to his name. He determined for a seven-year deal, one million dollars was not worth what it would cost him.

Master P played to his strengths of keeping business expenses down as he expanded his profit margins. For instance, he creatively employed guerrilla marketing by selling his music out of the trunk of his car in every city where there was potential demand for his music. Additionally, he gave out free music samples to the trendsetters in the neighborhood—those driving expensive cars. He knew they would drive their cars around to show them off, while bumping music from the No Limit label. Master P focused on branding all albums so the brand became more important than the actual artist's name. This consistent practice attracted more attention from distribution companies and others in the music industry.

Without money, marketing, or national distribution, Master P used his business acumen combined with his knowledge of the streets and hip-hop culture as his top strength to become one of the most successful independent artists of the nineties. Master P's experience demonstrates how accepting barriers can help accentuate one's strengths. He signed a music distribution deal with Priority Records, where No Limit Records would retain 100 percent ownership of their master recordings and keep 85 percent of their record's sales, while giving Priority 15 percent in return for pressing and distribution. This allowed No Limit to profit from future sales such as catalogs and reissues.

Master P went on to make hundreds of millions of dollars from this deal alone; he didn't even need to tour, which most artists must do to generate income. From 1997 to 2000, the label dropped fifty-one albums. In 1998, No Limit Records sold nearly fifteen million albums in one year, which had never been accomplished by rap artists from the South who did not crossover into the mainstream. Master P embraced his barriers, which allowed him to display his internal strengths and his Me Power. As shown by Master P's journey, it was the barriers that presented opportunities for him to grow and level up. He made a choice to embrace these barriers, which paid off in dividends, monetary and for his personal development.

From Juliet Cody's story about losing her eyesight in her forties, to Denzel Washington's struggle with school, to Master P's long journey to success, we takeaway that we can either look outside for help, find a solution from within, or do nothing when life throws us a curveball. These barriers may bring out weaknesses, but they may also create the conditions under which we can exercise Me Power and choose to leverage our strengths to keep moving forward.

DEFEAT INEVITABLE OBSTACLES ON THE PATH TO YOUR SUCCESS

Think of barriers as *temporary* obstacles. They separate you from your goal, whatever it may be. People err when they think of a barrier as something to be avoided at all costs. That's the wrong way to look at them.

Barriers are the steppingstones on the path to your dreams. They give you the first taste of how hard or easy that first step will be. Depending on the size of the stone, they can slow your progress or make you think your path is cut off by some obstacle impossible to pass. The point is, the obstacles in our way cannot stop us from doing amazing things if we use them as props to take us farther than we thought possible. Then, we can step on the stones that once blocked us and stand triumphantly.

You can't climb a mountain until you've reached the bottom.

At different points in our life, we will have obstacles, blockades, and impediments that stand in the way of our dreams, goals, and aspirations. Sometimes they're physical, like when you can't reach something because it's too high or too far away. Sometimes they're mental, like when you feel like giving up because you think you'll never meet your goal. We tend to internalize barriers—we think there's something wrong with us when we can't do something or that we'll never be able to do something because of a barrier.

But here's the thing: There's nothing wrong with barriers. And sometimes, barriers are precisely what you need to propel yourself forward.

Why? Because every time you encounter a barrier, it presents an opportunity to figure out how to get around it—or over it, or under it! It allows you to be creative in finding solutions to problems that might otherwise seem impossible to solve. And when we can do that, we build new skill sets and develop new ways of thinking about our potential as human beings—and that is the kind of learning that can truly change our lives forever.

Barriers give us a chance to test ourselves, to push ourselves beyond our comfort zone, and to see how much we want something. They force us out of our comfort zones to learn how to step into new ones—ones where we might just find some fantastic things waiting for us.

Obstacles are inevitable but never insurmountable.

FROM PRINCIPLE TO PRACTICE: EMBRACE YOUR BARRIERS

Let's use the secret weapon in our DNA, our reticular activating system (RAS), to our advantage. In *Insider*, Tony Robbins talks about using ten-minute priming rituals to bring mindfulness to one's endeavors, explaining, "the brain is not designed to make you happy. It's designed to make you survive. It's always looking for what's wrong." Because humans have a negativity bias built into our navigation of the world, we need to train our brains to our advantage. To do this, you could strengthen your RAS by:

- Saying your goals out loud;
- Imagining yourself achieving your goals;
- Disrupting negative thinking patterns with powerful questions and focusing on the positive;
- Looking at images of what you want; and/or
- Visualizing each step toward achieving your goal.

There is nothing more powerful than the way you ask a question, especially as you battle automatic negative thoughts (ANTs). My experience with Professor Obich was a single event that presented a seemingly insurmountable barrier. I identified an ANT that took me a long time to question. I was rejected from a doctoral program at an Ivy League and Professor Obich didn't think I was good enough to conduct academic research and writing. I internalized her thoughts and believed, "I'm a terrible student—a nonintellectual busy bee."

I began to disrupt my negative thoughts about the possibility of accomplishing my lifelong goal of obtaining a doctorate, with the question, "Am I condemning my entire life and goals on the basis of a single event?" By answering this powerful question in the affirmative, I began to see that just because the doctoral program did not accept me did not mean I was all the things Professor Obich said I was.

Embracing your barriers is key to using motivated energy to excel. When we feel motivated and energized we can overcome anything. To cultivate motivated energy, find a purpose you truly believe in. Remember to:

- Identify a clear purpose. Make it something you genuinely care about.
- Set measurable and achievable goals. Set yourself up to succeed with clear goals you know you can meet.
- Be ambitious. Don't set your goals too low—have faith in yourself and what you can achieve.
- Once you've tapped into your knowledge of self, think beyond yourself. Motivation only lasts so long when we focus solely on ourselves. Think about how your mission will help others and you'll tap into a new well of motivation.

Here are three additional exercises to help embrace your barriers as exciting challenges that fuel your motivated energy.

1. **Identify your blind spots.** Write down all your pet peeves and negative triggers in a notebook over the course of one week. What annoyed you? Frustrated you? Made you feel angry? Why?
2. **Write a letter to your future self and put it in a time capsule.** Set a date in your calendar and open it. In the letter, you can ask yourself, "What do I want to change within myself after nine months?"
3. **Call out your inner critic**, who sometimes runs silently in the background and takes over our thoughts unconsciously. Video or audio record your answer to the question, "What does that MF have to say to you?" Wait forty-eight hours to watch or listen to your inner

critic, then assume a power pose with your arms raised in a V-shape over your head. In your strongest voice, record a video or audio message telling your inner critic all the ways in which they are WRONG. Write these down as affirmations and say them in front of a mirror out loud every day for twenty-one days. Note the difference(s) in how you feel.

CHAPTER 5

FOCUS ON YOUR STRENGTHS (MY EDUCATION)

Our deepest fear is not that we are inadequate. Our deepest fear is that we are powerful beyond measure. It is our light, not our darkness, that most frightens us. We ask ourselves, "Who am I to be brilliant, gorgeous, talented, fabulous?" Actually, who are you not to be? You are a child of God. Your playing small doesn't serve the world. There's nothing enlightened about shrinking so that other people won't feel insecure around you. We were born to make manifest the glory of God that is within us. It's not just in some of us; it's in everyone. And as we let our own light shine, we unconsciously give other people permission to do the same. As we are liberated from our own fear, our presence automatically liberates others.

—MARIANNE WILLIAMSON

"Anyone can become disabled at any time," Haben Girma explained to the *Wall Street Journal.*

In 2013, Girma became the first deaf-blind person to graduate from Harvard Law School. As the daughter of an immigrant from Ethiopia and a refugee from Eritrea, her story is remarkable. She works as a human rights lawyer advancing disability justice; her work on *National Federation of the Blind v. Scribd* set a legal precedent requiring every American online business to comply with the Americans with Disabilities Act (ADA).

Highlighting the importance of accessibility as a legal right and good business practice, Girma explains, "You want to still be able to access your products and services even when your body changes, and all of our bodies change as we age."

Scribd, one of the world's largest Internet-based libraries in the world, published websites and mobile apps inaccessible to blind people. The blind use computers, smartphones, and tablets equipped with special software that allows the content of websites, mobile apps, and documents to be read aloud or displayed on a connected Braille device. When websites, mobile apps, or documents are not properly coded, they cannot be accessed with the technology used by the blind. This means thousands of books were missing from the libraries of those who could not afford expensive Braille devices or software. A judge ruled Scribd's failure to make its services available to blind people who access its website or mobile apps violated the ADA.

One of Girma's strengths is her belief that no feat is unconquerable, reflecting her powerful sense of self and determination. She does not feel she has limits in life and she believes the only limits that exist are the ones we place upon ourselves. Her life is a testament to a robust Me Power perspective. Her advocacy work challenges us to examine our unexamined ableist biases and practices. Ableist biases and practices enable and propagate the marginalization of people with disabilities. Rejecting the idea that she is an "inspiration cliche" and that deaf-blindness is something to "overcome," Girma explains, "The biggest barrier I face is ableism, the widespread beliefs, and practices that value nondisabled people over disabled people." In 2013, President Obama named her a White House Champion of Change, an award created as an opportunity for the White House to recognize citizens doing extraordinary things to empower members of their communities. She also received the Helen Keller Achievement Award and was recognized in *Forbes* 30 Under 30 and *TIME100 Talks*.

The fact that Girma advocates for the family and community that uplifted her also reflects (Our) Me Power.

Her sense of purpose to become a lawyer and advocate was resolute early on in life. Her parents supported her when many members of their community failed to comprehend how she would be able to attend college, due to the prevalent stereotype that deaf-blindless automatically precludes someone from attending college.

During her manifestation of Me Power, Girma exemplifies the second principle in practice: Focus On Your Strengths.

Deeply rooted in knowledge of self, focusing on your strengths provides the foundation for My Education, which includes learning within and beyond school. Beginning with a broad definition of strengths as a combination of our natural talents, inclinations, and values we can see in action, it is paramount to move beyond limitations and barriers by leveraging our strengths. With tools, we can identify what our strengths are, which provide much-needed insights to hidden potential deep within us. It is important to identify these strengths and use them as our own superpowers to get from where we are now to where we want to be in the future.

MY EDUCATION (ME) POWER

The *me* component associated with the second Me Power principle, Focus On Your Strengths, is My Education.

In Chapter 3, I discuss how education is more than formal schooling. Everything in your life, from what you do in school and at home, to what you do online or with friends, counts as education. For many people, education is about what you know and not who you are. When you think of education as more than just training and obtaining information, you free yourself and can focus on the learning-unlearning-relearning processes. Focusing on the cyclic nature of learning helps you to free yourself from the limiting idea that education is a linear process and can occur only in particular environments.

Aleen Jendian, my ninth-grade English teacher, is a brilliant educator who had a profound impact on my life.

Ms. Jendian and I met twenty-four years ago in her first year of teaching at Helix Charter High School. When she spoke, her eyes lit up and a smile spread across her face. I found myself grinning back, drawn in by her positivity. Whenever I walked into her classroom, I felt welcomed by the warmth of her smile and inviting gaze.

She was energetic and moved around the classroom a lot. Each day we met for ninety minutes on a block schedule, so she took time to meet individually with each student to get to know us better. This gave her insight into our interests and allowed her to find out what we liked to recommend books for us to read. She truly started with who we were as people before she emphasized anything she thought we needed to learn.

Ms. Jendian did a lot to position herself as a learner, sharing with us what she read and new things she learned. I felt electrified walking into her classroom because of the connections she made between what she learned and what we learned. Her passion for teaching, learning, and the human condition inspired me to be a better student and person. Her influence on me was so great, it later led me to choose a career in the field of education.

When I requested to interview Ms. Jendian for this book, asking her to discuss her perspectives on empowerment and its importance in education, she was shocked I would consider her an expert on the topic. But I knew that if anyone was going to speak from a heart-level perspective about empowerment and its importance in education, it would be Ms. Jendian. I had my own experiences with her as a student, then later as a colleague, but I wanted to capture her thoughts on the true meaning of empowerment.

After twenty-five years, Ms. Jendian continues to impress me with her ability to connect with students and teachers, her emphasis on knowing one's strengths, and demonstrating how such strengths could make their lives better by empowering themselves. She taught me about the importance of empowerment in education. She also gave me insight into what it means to truly empower oneself and others. She has dedicated her life to empowering others by teaching them to believe in themselves and their potential. That's why it was so important for me to include Ms. Jendian's perspectives on this topic in my first book—because they're real, honest, and grounded in what matters most: helping people focus on their strengths to manifest Me Power, so they can live their best lives.

At the beginning of our interview, Ms. Jendian explains the "[Latin] root of education, *educere*, means 'to draw forth.' Since I first learned this, it has been a huge part of my philosophy of teaching. Luckily, throughout my career, I've been at a school where they also believe that. You give students that high challenge and high support, and through your support, combined with the challenging environment, they're able to draw forth their academic strengths and curiosities."

Ms. Jendian's discussion about the root of education reminds me of an etymological debate about the meaning of education. Researchers (Craft, 1984 and Bass & Good, 2004) note there are two different Latin roots for the word: *educare*—to train or to mold—and *educere*—what Ms. Jendian explained. These meanings represent two different concepts. Every educator has the task of balancing the need to pass down knowledge and preparing a new generation for unknown changes on the horizon.

Ms. Jendian and I begin our conversation with this frame to make clear what education is and how the true meaning of empowerment, Me Power, is embedded within students taking charge of their own learning triad of unlearning, learning, and relearning. Ms. Jendian continues, "For me in the classroom, empowerment is everything. And I have two quotes that really capture it better than I will ever say." Ms. Jendian reads James Baldwin's "A Talk to Teachers" every year, where she incorporates his words into her teaching philosophy:

> *The purpose of education, finally, is to create in a person the ability to look at the world for himself, to make his own decisions, to say to himself this is black or this is white, to decide for himself whether there is a God in heaven or not. To ask questions of the universe, and then learn to live with those questions, is the way he achieves his own identity.*

Describing how reading Baldwin helps her practice Me Power, Ms. Jendian says, "This idea of drawing forth—empowering—allows and challenges students to draw forth on their strengths and ability to think critically, and gives them the tools in which to do that. I think that is the number one way I understand empowerment and education."

Ms. Jendian shares her passion for teaching students in a way that facilitates a dialectical process of empowerment: "I want them to see their strengths, and I want them to view themselves as capable. I can't do that *for* them, but I'll be there every step of the way as they recognize and develop their strengths. They have to recognize what they're capable of on their own. They have to see that learning is a process, and they have to find out what's missing."

At this moment in our interview, my thoughts flashed back to those moments in ninth-grade English class when Ms. Jendian would provide opportunities for us to figure out our strengths and then showcase them in class. She introduced me to the hero's journey in my ninth-grade honors English class, after reading *The Odyssey*, excerpts from Joseph Campbell's work, writing our reflections in dialectical journals, and then connecting the topic to *Star Wars*. In her class, I discovered my passion for research and writing and how to connect the dots between different disciplines.

For one's education, within or beyond the classroom, strengths are paramount to empowerment. For one's empowerment, it is essential to be aware of their own strengths. My Education begins with a strong foundation of *you*. Ms. Jendian encourages people to shift their thinking about empowerment, from a passive state to an active one. She explains, "Empowerment sounds like something's happening to you. But Me Power feels like, 'I'm doing more of it.' It's putting more of the responsibility on me. Me Power helps me focus on my strengths and how I can contribute those to society, which releases some pressure without forgoing responsibility. My larger philosophy of life is we're here to better the world around us. Whatever or however that may be for us depends on our own power. We need to own [(Our) Me Power] and use it for the good of humanity."

THE HARD PART ABOUT FOCUSING ON YOUR STRENGTHS IS THAT YOU HAVE TO FOCUS ON THEM

We tend to focus on the negative more than the positive, even when it's a matter of life and death. Psychologists call this tendency the negativity bias and it's a survival mechanism. In a situation where we must choose between focusing on a protective detail or an insidious detail, we'll choose what could kill us over what could only make us a little sick. And thanks to our tendency to remember bad things more than good ones, it means that we have a genetic predisposition to walk around every day with an awful-first-impression-is-the-last-impression perspective on life.

You can think of these negative thoughts as what Dr. Daniel G. Amen, clinical neuroscientist and psychiatrist, calls "automatic negative thoughts," or ANTs. In *Change Your Brain, Change Your Life*, Amen describes negative thoughts as pests that need to be exterminated: "Negative thoughts invade your mind like ants at a picnic." Pests, he says, seem to come out at the most inconvenient times—when you're trying to sleep, eat dinner, or have a conversation with someone. Similarly, our negative thoughts inevitably arise when we're in the middle of something else and we don't want them around.

We all have automatic negative thoughts. We're not always aware of them, but they operate in the back of our minds. These thoughts come from our beliefs and values and they form a lens through which we see the world. This can be an immense advantage when it comes to navigating complex situations. We must make decisions based on uncertain future outcomes and hasty responses are rarely the best options. But sometimes this mental process leads us down a path where we don't have all the information to make a good decision or choice. Unlike the ants we are all familiar with, these ANTs are dangerous because they can be self-fulfilling.

We must exterminate our ANTs to focus on our strengths. First, when you notice an ANT entering your mind, recognize it, write it down, and talk back to it. Second, when you hear yourself say an ANT, stop and course correct. Lastly, identify your most persistent ANTs and use this process to get rid of them. To truly exterminate ANTs, you must replace them with more positive and affirming thoughts.

Failing to check our ANTs can have a huge impact on how we make decisions and even our physical health. We must be aware of the negative consequences of holding onto false beliefs, such as not seeing the world as it really is, missing out on the wealth of information around us, and reacting to a very narrow view of things. The other side of any negative thought is a more positive possibility. In fact, every ANT has two parts: its direct opposite and a more subtle "shadow" that often goes unnoticed.

The direct opposite to every negative thought is its healthy counterpart or the positive way to view the situation at hand. For example, when you give someone an unexpected gift, you might automatically think they will say something critical about it. The direct opposite is your belief they will say something positive about it.

Take another example: you receive an email from your boss saying, "We need to talk about how things are going." What do you automatically assume? Do you assume he or she is thrilled with your work? Or do you assume he or she has noticed you've been making some mistakes lately and will call you into their office to reprimand you, or at the very worst, fire you? If your mind goes to the latter option, then you're probably setting yourself up for a psychological ANT hill by assuming the worst without even knowing if it's true.

To approach the situation better, say to yourself, "Okay, I'm sure there's a reason my boss wants to talk to me. Maybe they've noticed I've been working hard and doing some great things lately." When this happens, take a moment to notice your reaction. I guarantee when we take a moment and see the other side of an ANT, we will think something much more positive than what we originally thought when that red flag entered our minds.

By not exterminating our ANTs we operate from half-truths, which get in the way of focusing on our strengths.

You don't see the world as it really is. You miss out on the wealth of information around you and instead react to a very narrow view of things. The other half of any negative thought is a more positive possibility. Once these pests are removed, you see yourself in a completely different light and become an entirely new person with new goals.

We all have our own strengths but it can be hard to see them. This is especially true in the workplace, where we tend to focus on our weaknesses or what we don't like doing. However, when we look at our strengths, we can identify what we do well and what we enjoy, which encourage us to take pride in ourselves and build self-confidence.

One of the things that holds us back from realizing our strengths is that they are often less tangible than our weaknesses. In fact, many times they might not even be easily defined because we disguise them as something else. For example, a person who has a lot of energy and gets bored easily might just assume she's just hyperactive without ever considering her energy could translate into being an awesome teacher or athletic coach. A person who loves organizing things might assume he has OCD instead of realizing his love for organization makes him a perfect event planner. As these examples show, it can be difficult for people to identify their own strengths because it requires them to look beyond cultural assumptions and stereotypes, which are things outside of them they cannot control.

Once you know your strengths, you can harness them to reach your goals and enhance your Me Power.

DEFINE STRENGTHS: BREADTH BEFORE DEPTH

Before I discuss how to identify your strengths, it is important to define what I mean by strengths. I define strengths in a broad way, including your natural talents, inclinations, relationships, resources, reputation, skills, ability to work in certain contexts, and character traits.

When deciding what your strengths are, the first step is to define "strength" as broadly as possible. If you narrow your perspective too soon, you won't be able to see all the potential ways strengths can come into play. To begin, try brainstorming a short list of things that come to your mind when someone asks about your strengths. Think about all the roles you play in life and include anything that comes up. Then look over the list and ask yourself two questions: "When you employ your strengths, such as creativity or motivating others in a meeting, how does it make you feel?" and "Do you feel energized and empowered, or do you feel drained and exhausted?" Consider all facets of your life: family and friends, hobbies and leisure time activities, work life, relationships with coworkers and supervisors—basically anything that contributes to your sense of identity.

Our strengths reflect the essence of who we are. They make us unique and we can leverage our strengths to help us Embrace Our Barriers and overcome obstacles.

THE FIRST STEP TO LEVERAGING YOUR STRENGTHS IS IDENTIFYING THEM

Everyone has some form of strengths blindness. This phenomenon occurs when you're so used to doing something, you cannot see it from the perspective of someone else who does not have your particular strength. Strengths blindness can cause you to underestimate your own strengths and the strengths of others. Sometimes, you don't see the ways in which your strengths can positively impact your life and the lives of others.

For example, let's say you are good at remembering things, like my husband, Dave, who has had to memorize numerous drug interactions in his fifteen-year career as a pharmacist. You carry a lot on your plate and have never had an issue with remembering everything that was due when it was due. However, you start working with a new assistant who always seems to forget things. This can certainly be frustrating for you because you are used to being organized and staying on top of things. You may not understand why this person cannot keep up with you. This is a case where your strengths blindness kicks in, making it hard for you to see how a strength you take for granted may be difficult for someone else.

The best way to overcome strengths blindness is by learning how you use your strengths differently than others use theirs—meaning each person's perceived weakness may actually be their greatest strength.

Two-thirds of people have no idea what their strengths are but a growing body of evidence suggests developing strengths at work is key to unleashing our personal and professional success. (Biswas-Diener et al., 2011; Lawn & Mapp, 2014; Niemiec & McGrath, 2019) By failing to focus on your strengths and leverage them, you miss out on the key to success and manifesting Me Power. It is most important, however, to learn how to recognize your gifts and then work with them. The answers to this all start with self-knowledge: you must first be aware of who you are and what you can do to get the most out of yourself and your life.

To leverage your strengths, you must first identify what they are. This is easier said than done because we often don't know what our strengths are or choose to ignore them, fearing that others might call us arrogant or boastful. In fact, many people were told as children they are special or have gifts but were never actually taught how to use those gifts or talents for their benefit. The good news is there are several ways you can begin the process of identifying your strengths. After brainstorming your own list, you can also ask people who know you well, like family members, friends, and coworkers, what they think your strengths are.

According to *The Power of Character Strengths,* nine out of ten people find it much easier to spot strengths in others. (Niemiec and McGrath, 2019) You can use the SEA acronym as a framework to have someone else spot your strengths. You can use the SEA framework to acknowledge the link between strengths and behaviors:

- **S**pot: Label the strength you see in a friend, relative, or coworker. Is it a strength from CliftonStrengths or the Values in Action (VIA) Survey you recognize?

- **E**xplain: Describe the strength you see and the reason behind it when you talk to them.
- **A**ppreciate: Tell them what their strength means to you and the value it brings.

THREE TOOLS TO DISCOVER YOUR STRENGTHS

While the work of developing one's strengths can be daunting, the tools available to help us along the way are abundant and easy to understand. To leverage your strengths, you must first broadly define strength, then identify yours and understand what they are using tools such as Myers-Briggs Type Indicator, Values in Action (VIA) Survey, and/or CliftonStrengths. These three tools not only help to discover your strengths but also help you develop your Me Power, a combination of your self-knowledge and principled action of Focus On Your Strengths.

MYERS-BRIGGS

The Myers-Briggs Type Indicator (MBTI) is one of many personality assessments that help individuals to better understand themselves and appreciate others. Taking a free version online may be helpful, but you'll get the most out of the MBTI if you have a certified professional administer it and interpret your results. Your "score" on the test is the combination of the four characteristics indicated by self-reported answers. There are sixteen personality types defined by four traits:

- Introversion (I) and Extraversion (E), which refer to where an individual gets his or her energy from;
- Intuition (N) and Sensing (S), which refer to how individuals perceive the world around them;
- Feeling (F) and Thinking (T), which refer to how an individual makes decisions; and
- Judging (J) and Perceiving (P), which refer to how individuals relate to the environment.

According to the Myers-Briggs Company, about 1.5 million people take the MBTI online each year and more than 88 percent of Fortune 500 companies and hundreds of universities use it in hiring and training. People have criticized the MBTI because it lacks predictive validity, meaning it doesn't predict what people will do in the future. In *Psychology Today*, licensed psychologist and psychology professor Dr. Aqualus Gordon explains, "A common misunderstanding of the MBTI is that it predicts job performance. It does not. However, personality type does seem to have a significant association with school and career *preference* and *satisfaction*."

VALUES IN ACTION SURVEY OF CHARACTER STRENGTHS

In *Character Strengths and Virtues*, positive psychologists Christopher Peterson and Martin Seligman, identify six core virtues comprising twenty-four positive parts of your personality that make you feel authentic and engaged. The organization of the six virtues and twenty-four strengths is as follows:

- **Wisdom and Knowledge:** Creativity, Curiosity, Open-Mindedness, Love of Learning, Perspective;
- **Courage:** Bravery, Persistence, Integrity, Zest;
- **Humanity:** Love, Kindness, Social Intelligence;
- **Justice:** Teamwork, Fairness, Leadership;
- **Temperance:** Forgiveness and Mercy, Humility, Prudence, Self-Control; and
- **Transcendence:** Appreciation of Beauty and Excellence, Gratitude, Hope, Humor, Spirituality

To operationalize these virtues, Seligman and a team of researchers created the Values in Action Inventory of Strengths, now known as the VIA Survey. The VIA Survey is a psychometrically validated assessment that ranks these twenty-four character strengths in a unique profile. The twenty-four measured character strengths have been found to be universal across countries, cultures, and beliefs. To date, over twenty-one million people have taken the VIA Survey.

There are three main reasons why character strengths matter. First, they are essential to well-being. Second, they facilitate an individual's ability to live and work in accordance with their ideals. Third, they enable an individual to be a better friend and partner, relative, or citizen. Character strengths are the key to unlocking a better, happier life and they are within every single one of us. It is important to identify your strengths and use them as your own superpowers to get from where you are now to where you want to be in the future. The VIA Survey is one of several tools that can help you focus on your strengths to manifest Me Power.

GALLUP CLIFTONSTRENGTHS

The CliftonStrengths assessment is based on the research of Dr. Don Clifton and distributed by the Gallup Organization, most known for its public opinion polls conducted worldwide. For decades, Gallup has been a leader in the strengths movement with research into workplace outcomes, individual well-being, and employee performance and engagement. Over 90 percent of Fortune 500 companies have used the CliftonStrengths assessment to improve workplace relationships.

According to Gallup, there are 278,256 possible combinations of its top five themes, also known as Signature Strengths, and more than thirty-three million different sets of these, so each result is unique to you.

CliftonStrengths sorts its thirty-four talent themes into four domains:

- **Strategic Thinking**: Analytical, Context, Futuristic, Ideation, Input, Intellection, Learner, Strategic;
- **Executing**: Achiever, Arranger, Belief, Consistency, Deliberative, Discipline, Focus, Responsibility, Restorative;
- **Influencing**: Activator, Command, Communication, Competition, Maximizer, Self-Assurance, Significance, Woo; and

- **Relationship Building**: Adaptability, Connectedness, Developer, Empathy, Harmony, Includer, Individualization, Positivity, Relator.

After twenty-five million completed assessments, Gallup researchers (Asplund & Hickman, 2021) found:

- race, gender, and nationality indicate almost nothing about a person's strengths;
- strengths affect team performance, especially when they're coached; and
- a strengths-based philosophy improves employee engagement for stronger performance outcomes.

Asplund and Hickman (2021) end the report by asking: "What would happen to companies if a billion people were coached to use their strengths to their full potential, instead of trying to 'fix' their weaknesses? What would happen to engagement if a billion people worked in roles or for organizations that embrace their strengths?"

These three tools help us discover strengths. Sometimes, we get so lost in our own lives we don't even realize where we're headed or recognize our strengths, too focused on fixing what's wrong. What if I told you your path is right in front of you? That the answers are inside of you, and all it takes is a little bit of digging to find them?

You see, people search for a goldmine outside of themselves—in their careers, their relationships, their bank accounts—but really they're looking in all the wrong places. When they tap into their Me Power, they realize they have always had everything they needed.

Focusing on our strengths allows us to move away from complaints toward concentration and action. It's easy to complain and people often do it unconsciously. Vent as much as you need to. It's essential to let off steam as a healthy way of coping with stress and dissatisfaction. Also known as catharsis, venting plays a major role in psychotherapy and is the single most common reason for complaining in social interactions.

But once you get it out, don't keep complaining about the same things. When you complain, you only focus on what's holding you back. It's a disadvantage to focus on what seems insurmountable because it makes you feel like you don't have the power to change things. But if you can get in the habit of looking for your strengths instead of your drawbacks, you'll be sure to move from a place of frustration and helplessness to a place of action.

Your focus determines your reality. In other words, *you* are in charge of your life. What you focus on expands. Your life reflects what you choose to focus on, so choose wisely. To live your best life, you must choose focus over distraction. Be conscious of your focus. Think about where you put your attention; ask yourself what you are going to do with that focus. By identifying your strengths, you can build upon your strengths, leverage your unique superpowers, and manifest Me Power as you deepen self-knowledge and principled action.

FROM PRINCIPLE TO PRACTICE: FOCUS ON YOUR STRENGTHS

How do you know your strengths? You must first broaden your definition of strengths and then identify them, by asking yourself and others questions like the following:

- What am I good at?
- What's the weirdest thing about me, an unusual skill or talent, that also benefits someone else?
- What are my hobbies and activities that allow me to shine?
- When I feel most successful, what makes me feel that way?
- If I could do anything in the world, what would I be doing?
- What do people say I do best?

Please take a free, scientifically validated Values in Action (VIA) assessment of your strengths. The VIA Survey is available on my website at www.lanysha.com, where you can take it by clicking "FOCUS ON YOUR STRENGTHS" or scanning the QR code below. You can retake the VIA Survey every six months, allowing you to monitor your growth, identify areas for improvement, and take principled action to boost your Me Power.

India Nixon-Lyon, MBA, business owner, and a dear friend of mine, said these encouraging words to me as I struggled to finish *Me Power*. It's a wonderful exercise that will leave you feeling energized and invigorated, encouraging you to use your strengths every day:

Take a walk around your space,
Step outside for a moment,
Stretch to the sky,
Bend over to touch your toes,
Make silly faces at yourself in the mirror and laugh out loud,
Think about your strengths as a superpower when you're at your best,
Focus on the YOU that shines and radiates brilliance.

What is one thing that you've wanted to do that someone said you couldn't or blocked you from doing?

1. Write that down, using language to express possibility and your intentions.
2. Now ask yourself, in what ways did their blocking actually serve you? Create a list.
3. Now, take a look at that list and think of the ways in which what they said or did was not true.
4. On a new sheet of paper, write that down.
5. Read the list and think about how what is written there is not true.
6. Burn or destroy the first list somehow.
7. Celebrate that feeling of releasing the negative hold those thoughts and emotions have on you.

8. With the remaining list, for every point, add a strength you have that supports what you wrote. Smile after reading each point.
9. Spend a week finding a way to exercise each of these strengths in the world.
10. After a week, reflect and document (write, audio or video record, paint, dance) your use of those strengths. Connect these to one of your signature strengths, noting evidence of it.
11. Repeat the process until you believe it. Be the results.

For example, I might take Professor Obich's decision to reject my application for the doctoral program as a sign that I could not succeed in a Ph.D. program:

On the first sheet of paper, I'd write, "I will get my PhD."

Underneath that, I'd start listing why I believed what Professor Obich said was correct.

- Because of where you come from, people like you are not suited for intellectual activity.
- Your place in the world is to work as hard as your enslaved ancestors did before you.
- Because you're Black, there's no way you will be in the academy—look around!

After reading each point I accept the fact that none of these reasons will stop me from earning my doctorate. I visualize the day I will walk across the stage to get hooded. I see the conferred degree in my hand weeks later. I frame the degree and hang it up where I see it every day. "LaNysha T. Adams, Doctor of Philosophy." I smile, thinking about the fact that my teenage dream, seemingly impossible, is now my reality.

With renewed energy, on a new sheet of paper, I write down the ways in which the previous points are not true:

- You just accepted a job as a research director, a role you earned based on your excellent ideas and skills in conducting research, writing reports, and presenting them.
- Working hard is valuable, but I get to choose the work I love to build the life I want. I praise and thank my ancestors. I am my future ancestor.
- I can be a tenured professor despite the fact only 2 percent of Black women are tenured professors.

CHAPTER 6

SPEAK FOR YOUR LIFE (MYSELF EXPRESSED)

I want to remind you that all things material come from the invisible field of the immaterial, beyond space and time. Simply said, by planting seeds in this world, you see that in time they bear fruit. If you can experience a dream so completely in mind and emotion within the inner world of potentials, then it has already happened. So just surrender; it has to sprout into your outer life. It is the law.

—DR. JOE DISPENZA

Have you ever planted a seed in your backyard or in a pot on your windowsill? What happened?

You planted it, nurtured it, and hopefully, watched it grow. Your care created a new life.

When you plant the seed of an idea in your own mind, you give yourself new life to explore and experience. Once the seed is planted it begins to take shape. When you speak your idea out loud or write it down, it starts to take shape and grow. It brings with it new experiences and opportunities. There's nothing quite like having a conversation with someone else about an idea you carry around inside your head. It can be exhilarating to share what you feel and think with others. By setting your "seed" free into the world, you express yourself. In addition, the "seed" finds fertile soil when connecting with others, where it can sprout and grow into something beautiful.

The law that Dr. Dispenza describes, of planting seeds first, then waiting for them to bear fruit, is a kind of creation where life is created twice. First, we think about it and then we make it so.

What if you could make your most positive thoughts a reality?

That's the promise of the third principle of Me Power, expressed in the command Speak for Your Life. It means taking full responsibility for what happens in your life and literally calling it out, speaking life into existence. The way you speak will create the life you live. Therefore, it's important to find your authentic voice and use it to express your ideas, views, and desires in a variety of settings and mediums. Speaking for your life means finding what you want to say, then saying it—with language and/ or other forms of expression and with honesty, openness, and vulnerability. Speak for Your Life means speaking up for your authentic self, engaging in positive self-talk, and honoring the responsibility that comes with being heard and understood.

MY SELF, EXPRESSED (ME) POWER

The *me* component associated with Speak for Your Life is Myself Expressed.

A person can never be reduced to a single version of themselves. We are not static beings—we grow, we evolve, and our identities shift over the course of our lives. Each version of ourselves is a new way for us to express who we truly are. We constantly change in response to the contexts we encounter. A commitment to knowing ourselves and the multiple versions of self we create is about engaging in a learning triad of unlearning, learning, and relearning over time. Even when we are at the end of our lives, we still change.

My maternal grandfather, the late L. T. Stanley Jr., or Paw-Paw as my family and I always called him, is a perfect example of someone who embodied the third Me Power principle. He was born in Broken Arrow, Oklahoma on October 30, 1937. A son of the late Ida Mae Willis and L.T. Stanley Sr., L. T. appreciated his Native American roots in the Cherokee Nation. Never forgetting where he came from, L. T.'s favorite musical was *Oklahoma!*

After high school, he enlisted in the Navy and served as a coxswain at Pearl Harbor. He helped transport visitors safely to and from the USS Arizona Memorial, where over one million people visit each year to pay their respects to the men who lost their lives in the attack.

The three words I use to describe L. T. are consistent, punctual, and dedicated. After serving in the Navy, he worked as a shipping and receiving clerk for forty years at the largest department store chain on the West Coast, Carter Hawley Hale Stores, for which he received an "Outstanding Service" award. Described by his best friends as always "suited and booted with a hat," he literally spoke *for* his life, expressing his Me Power.

"I really need to speak with you," my grandfather implored over the phone.

"I wish I could come out, but I can't because it's the pandemic. We can talk on the phone and even video chat, Paw-Paw."

"I have no privacy! I need to speak with you in person. How soon can you get here?"

As I held my three-month-old son Donovan and watched his two-year-old brother Davidson line up dinosaurs on the couch next to us, I wondered if I could safely get to Los Angeles. My husband, David Foss, a Commissioned Corps Pharmacy Officer in the United States Public Health Service, was on an extended detail from his work at the FDA, distributing monoclonal antibodies to priority areas and helping establish Operation Warp SPEED (Special Project for Efficient and Equitable Distribution). According to the World Health Organization, over 32.7 million COVID-19 cases and 991,000 deaths had been reported at the end of September 2020.

I shook my head at the impossibility, deafened by the silence and uncertainty of if or when I would ever see my grandfather again.

"Sweetheart, how soon can you get here? I know the baby cannot wear a mask. Can Davidson?"

"I don't know how I would do it with them on my own during the pandemic, Paw-Paw."

While I considered visiting my grandfather, I remembered hearing about a child who became critically ill after waiting for treatment options. His doctor went through the bureaucratic process of obtaining permission from the drug company and the FDA for an emergency Investigational New Drug approval. My heart broke when I learned this boy had died.

"The sooner I can see you, the better. I'm not sure I..." The silence on the other end of the line was broken by his voice. It had a sad timbre that made my heart ache, but I was determined to let him know how much I wanted to see him before his inevitable departure.

My voice was hoarse and I could feel my throat closing up as these words left my mouth: "I can't make any promises, but I will look into seeing how I can visit you before the end of the year." It felt like he was sitting right next to me, so close that I could smell him and that familiar scent of Old Spice, which always reminded me of our time together.

My grandfather always did what he promised and as someone I admired, I also believed "your word is your bond." My grandfather's stage-five kidney failure and refused dialysis also motivated me to try to visit him.

After surviving COVID-19, he had several strokes and, subsequently, lost all mobility in his body. I determined his prognosis did not look good, especially since he was determined to speak with me. I felt an emotional panic arise as I tried to figure out how I could get to Southern California and see him.

"When was the last time I even went *anywhere*?" I asked myself aloud.

The last time my husband and I traveled, we took our Donovan—in utero—and Davidson on their first international trip to Europe and spent two weeks exploring the Netherlands and Belgium. We returned to the United States on Monday, March 9, 2020. The next day President Donald Trump announced the US would be closed to all flights from Europe to stop the spread of COVID-19 in the country.

Since then, the only places I had visited were my obstetrician and the hospital to give birth to Donovan on June 18, 2020. While contemplating traveling with two small children, I realized I needed a lot of things I did not have at the time:

- a dual stroller that was compact and sturdy enough to hold an infant and a forty-pound two year old;
- a large diaper bag with plenty of snacks, supplies, and airplane-friendly toys;
- a strategy for changing diapers on a plane without them touching everything;
- plane tickets on a nonstop flight;

- a travel breastfeeding pillow;
- a ride to the airport;
- a compact pack and play;
- a travel-friendly car seat for a tall toddler;
- knowledge of where to get COVID tested once we arrived; and
- a place to quarantine for at least five days after traveling and before testing, ahead of visiting the nursing care facility.

I resolved to carefully weigh my options for three days before taking any action. Each day during my 3 a.m. feeding sessions with Donovan, I felt overwhelmed by anticipating regret. The sorrow of not making an attempt to see my grandfather before he died brought me to my knees as I recited the Serenity Prayer (Crouter, 2010), until the tears stopped and I felt a quiet resolve.

God grant me the Serenity to accept the things I cannot change, Courage to change the things I can, and Wisdom to know the difference.

Dave, who had lost his last living grandparent a couple of years earlier, nodded in understanding when I told him, "I have to go."

"How will you manage to carry the baby, handle Davidson, and all the things they need? Will you be okay if he doesn't make it by the time you get there?" he asked.

"I don't know. I have to see my Paw-Paw. I'll figure the rest out somehow."

Wondering how high risk I was battling postpartum pre-eclampsia, a rare condition that occurs when you have high blood pressure soon after childbirth, I shared the news with my grandfather and felt his energy shift even though we were on the phone.

"Oh, I'm so happy! I need to speak to you without someone holding a phone, listening in. It's important."

"See you in November, Paw-Paw."

"I'm gonna hang on a while longer," he promised.

After we hung up, I booked two surprisingly inexpensive first-class tickets, one from Reagan National Airport to Las Vegas, and one red eye back from Los Angeles to Dulles. When Davidson licked the armrest, I almost lost it. This is precisely why I wondered if traveling with my infant and two-year-old son was worth a last-ditch effort to see my grandfather. In my mind, I replayed him asking me five separate times in one conversation to speak with me in person.

I found a nice apartment-style hotel off the Strip where we quarantined for five days, got tested, and received our results before visiting my grandfather's nursing care facility, Broadway by the Sea. My aunt, who lives in Vegas, offered support by bringing over my favorite home-cooked meals and drove us from Vegas to LA.

My grandfather was a man of few words. I was eager to find out which family secrets he would reveal before he passed. When the facility staff wheeled my grandfather out, my heart leaped. This was the moment I had been waiting for. I introduced him to Donovan, his youngest great-grandchild, and asked how he was doing. I sat there as the sun beamed down on us, thinking about how I escaped the colder temperatures of DC.

"So Paw-Paw, I'm here now. What did you need to tell me?"

He spoke in such a soft voice that I had to lean in to hear him, almost violating the social distance rule of six feet apart.

"I can't talk so loud. They might hear us," he whispered.

"Who?"

"Them," he signaled with his eyes. "They watch my every move and listen to everything I say."

I uncomfortably shifted in my seat. "Well, they're in there now so you have some time to tell me before they come back."

"What kind of car did you rent?"

I smiled at the question. He always asked me about the car I rented when I came to town, though it was always a different one. For forty-one years, you could tell L. T.

was present because of his red Chrysler Cordoba, which he meticulously kept as new as the day he bought it off the showroom floor in 1976.

"The white Toyota Camry over there."

"Perfect," he said. "Now while they're in there, load me up, and get me out of here!"

"What? How? Where will we go?" I laughed but also realized he was as serious as a sudden cardiac arrest.

"Just get me out of here while we can still go."

"Paw-Paw, I can't. I would have to load you, your chair, then the boys, and their stroller; it's a small sedan so I don't think we could all fit. Let's talk about something we can do, like what was so important to tell me that I had to come all this way during a global pandemic with two kids?"

"I need to get out of here."

This was the last time I'd see him alive.

My grandfather advocated for himself. He was determined to live his best life, even when it seemed like he wouldn't make it to see the end of the year. Even though I was unable to break him out of his nursing care facility, he expressed himself, commanding me to show up and help him escape. He spoke up for himself and showed how determined he was to live his life to the fullest.

At the end of his life, his voice was soft and sometimes hard to hear, but he spoke with confidence and without hesitation. He knew what he wanted and he wasn't afraid to ask for it, even if his words were slurred or hard to decipher. His ability to communicate in this way made me reflect on how important communication is to ensure our own autonomy, regardless of age or health status.

On May 12, 2021, L. T. Stanley Jr., my last living grandparent, passed away in Long Beach, California, at the age of eighty-three years old. His legacy, however, still lives on. From the stories of his past, to the memories I shared with him, and up to the final time I spent with him, he put his voice out into the world and spoke for his life from his heart, mind, and soul.

TELL THE WORLD WHO YOU ARE WITH PURPOSE

To Speak for Your Life, you have to define your purpose. You are the secret to defining your life.

"Begin with an end in mind," Stephen Covey writes in *The 7 Habits of Highly Effective People*. Okay death, here we are. That is the ultimate "end," in the here and now, or the "final" destination toward which all our efforts lead us. *Memento mori*, the Latin phrase to keep one's hubris in check, is a good call to action to remember death.

But how many of us think about life as something we construct on the pathway to our end? Or, perhaps worse yet, how many of us don't think about it at all?

Before one can begin building a life, he or she must define who they are. Our lives are always in the process of being built, so as long as there is breath in our bodies we must remain aware that our "most important work" is ahead of us, not behind us.

Let's do what Richie Norton recommends and just S.T.O.P., or "Start to Open Possibilities."

Knowing yourself and living with a well-defined purpose is key to experiencing a more meaningful life. A new learning triad with self-knowledge at the center, like deep learning, is "about transforming our reality through learning, both individually and with others."

In their study, Alimujiang and colleagues (2019) found individuals who have a purpose in life tend to be more resilient than those who do not. Their research suggests if you volunteer, have a therapist, meditate, and focus on mindfulness, you may decrease your chances of dying early because you are less likely to experience stress or depression resulting from negative thoughts about your life. Individuals who engage in volunteering and other activities that promote physical activity are most likely to report higher levels of purpose in life. These results show meaningful activities are important for exercising one's sense of purpose and improving mental and physical health.

The purpose of human life is to impact the world around you through the act of creation, taking action in a principled manner. The act of creation is not limited to painting, writing, or building; it can be anything that contributes to the well-being of others. The simplest way to activate (Our) Me Power is by doing something that makes someone else's life better based on your self-knowledge and principled action. You just have to do something unique to you that improves someone else's life in some way—whether it's helping them with their homework, giving them a ride when they need one, lending them money when they're down on their luck, or some other random act of kindness.

The Greek word *poiesis* describes this activation of Me Power.

According to Dr. Derek Whitehead (2003), the term has nothing to do with free will and everything to do with "the opening of a world for humankind's being and action. Poiesis means 'to produce into presence.' Such production becomes associated with *gnosis*, with 'knowing.'" We always aim to create. The clock starts at birth. Poiesis, then, is the activity of bringing something into being; it is a way of revealing and opening up; it is a kind of planting seeds that bear fruit over time.

Adam Leipzig has produced and supervised films that have won or been nominated for ten Academy Awards, eleven BAFTA Awards, two Golden Globes, two Emmys, two Directors Guild Awards, and four Sundance Awards. His TED Talk, "How to Know Your Life Purpose in Five Minutes" has over seventeen million views. He explains to find your purpose, you must ask yourself five questions:

- Who are you?
- What do you do? What are you best at?
- Who do you do it for? (e.g., family, parents, friends, wife, husband, etc.)
- What do those people want or need? Why do people come to you for the thing you do?
- What do those people get out of it or how do they change as a result of what you did?

(Our) Me Power, or the "we inside of me," is illustrated by Leipzig's question: "Now why is that formulation so powerful? Because of all those five things that you need to know to know what your life purpose is, only two are about yourself."

The Parable of the Sower in the Bible talks about a seed falling on four different soils. Truly a testament to how context is everything, the seeds are scattered in different places: on a path, on rocky ground, among thorns, and in good soil. Only on good soil will the seed produce fruit since the conditions under which the seeds fell determine whether they grew and how lasting and fruitful their growth was.

Remember what I mentioned at the beginning of this chapter about the seed, or the idea in your mind? We want our ideas to be the seed on good soil, not the seed the thorns choke, the seed that dries up in sun, or the seed eaten by the birds, nor the seed that sprouts for a little while but eventually dies. We want our ideas for life to be expressed, to grow in good soil, to be nourished with water and sunlight, and grow up strong and healthy. The best project you will ever work on is Y.O.U.—it's

Your Opportunity to go all the way *Up,* Speak for Your Life, and manifest Me Power.

How will you choose to Speak for Your Life?

FROM PRINCIPLE TO PRACTICE: SPEAK FOR YOUR LIFE

In her dissertation seeking to understand the reintegration experiences of formerly incarcerated African American men, pastor and scholar-activist Dr. Cathy Ames Turner (2022) asks, "If you were to write your life story, what would the title be?" What would the title of your life story be, dear reader? Why?

Jack Canfield, multiple *New York Times* bestselling author best known for *Chicken Soup for the Soul* series, which has more than 250 titles and five hundred million copies in print in over forty languages, outlines eight guidelines for creating affirmations:

1. Start with the words, "I am."
2. Use the present tense to imagine yourself being in the moment and experiencing the reality of your goal being achieved. This prompt will encourage you to take persistent action to make your vision real.
3. Say it out loud in a positive tone and with confidence.
4. Keep it brief so the affirmations are easy to memorize and repeat.
5. Make it specific. Daily affirmations such as, "I am so happy and grateful now that I've lost weight," aren't nearly as powerful as, "I am so happy and grateful

now that I have lost fifteen pounds and am wearing my favorite jeans again!"

6. Include an action word ending with "-ing." This allows you to express your affirmation as if you are experiencing it at that very moment. For example, "I am so happy and grateful to be walking across the stage to accept my master's degree from Columbia University." The more you can imagine yourself in that moment of walking across that stage, the more powerful your affirmation will be.

7. Include at least one dynamic emotion or feeling word.

8. Make affirmations for yourself, not others.

Susan Sontag writes, "In the journal, I do not just express myself more openly than I could to any person; I create myself." How is this true for you? Who were you before? Who are you today? Who will be in the future?

Write your obituary, focusing on what you have left to accomplish. This exercise may prompt you to ask, "What's missing from my life?" You may also wonder, "What do I need to do in order for my obituary to be complete?" Start by answering the following questions:

- What are you known for?
- How do you want to be remembered?
- What are some of your greatest accomplishments?
- What have you learned from your early years, early adulthood, and later years?
- Which three adjectives best describe you?
- What do you consider the highlights of your life apart from your family and career?

CHAPTER 7

CHOOSE YOUR GUIDE(S)
(MASTER EXCELLENCE)

You have a lot of power in your relationships. However, all of it has to do with how you choose to conduct yourself, because this is what lies within your realm of power. You can choose what you decide to do with the feelings you experience. You can choose how you treat others. You can choose how to live your life.

—LAURA MILTENBERGER

We cannot go through life alone.

There have been numerous experiments that support this, especially for children. While many think Mowgli from the *Jungle Book* by Rudyard Kipling is merely a fictional character, there are cases of feral children in real life, whose parents or guardians abandoned them to grow up in extreme isolation.

One of the most popular cases focuses on Genie from Los Angeles, who spent her entire childhood locked in a bedroom, isolated, and abused in the seventies. Serendipity struck when Genie's mother accidentally went to a social services office instead of an office to file for disability benefits. A social worker immediately picked up on Genie's cognitive abilities and she was taken from her abusive, neglectful parents. After she was taken from her parents, she immediately began a process of rehabilitation. Her linguistic progress, however, never advanced beyond putting a few words together. It was noted she did not produce any sentences showing mastery of English grammar.

Victor, the "Wild Boy of Aveyron," was also well-known for spending his life surviving in the forests of France alone at the end of the eighteenth century. I initially learned about Victor and Genie in a linguistics class at Cal State San Marcos, where we debated the innateness of language, the process of learning to speak, and if there was a critical age for acquiring language, even though Noam Chomsky asserts language acquisition is part of the human "genetic blueprint."

In 1800, researchers found twelve-year-old Victor and tried to civilize him. After several years, Victor learned to read and write simple sentences but never learned to speak. The doctor studying him closely, Dr. Jean Marc Gaspard Itard, made the grave error of equating speech with language: He never thought to teach Victor how to sign. We will never know the truth behind Victor or Genie's story. However, Roger Shattuck (1994), a National Book Award-winning scholar and author of one of the most prominent texts on "wild" children suggested,

"Victor and Genie probably suffered irreversible brain damage from isolation."

I selected these extreme examples to show human beings cannot survive without other people. Our very survival as a species depends on socialization. I cover this in depth in Chapter 2, where I explain (Our) Me Power as a kind of "we-ness" over "me-ness" you experience because of your ability to transcend individual circumstances and experience yourself as part of an interconnected whole—what Dr. Taylor calls "the 'we' inside of 'me.'" We are social creatures and our very survival as a species depends on it.

A study based on data from the Survey of Health, Aging, and Retirement in Europe spanning eleven European countries and thirty-one thousand individuals in twenty-two thousand households found individuals who participated in social or community activities reported excellent health over the age of fifty. Socialization is a key part of our individual development, no matter our age. Research indicates our genetic makeup and social environments both in which we are raised and those we live in as adults affect who we are.

From where you start, how do you know which way to go to get where you want to be? The answer is not always clear and we are often limited in our understanding of the myriad of possibilities. It is at this juncture that choosing a guide is essential.

We are the heroes of our own stories. We are not passive observers. We are not just spectators. We are not just along for the ride. We are active participants in our own lives and we can activate Me Power to live up to our full potential.

The fourth Me Power principle is Choose Your Guide(s). You cannot evolve beyond the level of your present state of consciousness without a guide of some kind. Friends, mentors, and coaches are all guides who may have been involved in your life. They challenge you and call you out, asking questions that allow you to develop a deeper understanding of yourself. Success is not only an individual accomplishment but also a reflection of all the people who have helped you over time. Remember you are the hero in your own story. Every hero has a guide. You may need a guide and you may also be someone else's guide on their heroic journey.

In this chapter, I define a guide as a kind of amplifier for your life and explain what a good guide looks like, using Monet and his pursuit to master excellence as a Me Power exemplar. Next, I will let you know a guide can act as an encourager or motivator and help you pave your way because they see things you have not yet experienced. Lastly, I explain the function of your guide and explain how choosing your guide is a vital part of your self-knowledge and principled action, or empowerment journey.

GUIDES AMPLIFY YOUR LIFE

As I define it here, a guide refers to any person who advises, shows the way, or influences your course of action. A guide is like an amplifier in that they improve performance, help you show your talent, help you become a better listener, increase the sound of your voice, and generate direction.

Amplifiers increase the voltage, current, or power of electrical signals. If a speaker is incorrectly connected to the amplifier, it may not play sound as loud as you wish. If a speaker isn't plugged into the proper outlet, it may experience problems with sound distortion. If a speaker is plugged into an improper outlet, the electricity running through the wires will be uneven and damage the speakers.

A guide is someone who knows your destination and understands your route, often from direct experience or insight. They have the skills to help you overcome obstacles, especially those hidden from view. Guides are people who help you see the path ahead of you, provide advice and support, and challenge you to be your best self.

Many think their parents are their de facto guides. However, a parent may not be an objective guide. The child may not align with the hopes and wishes the parent holds for them, making it difficult for parents to clearly see and support their divergent path of interest.

That's why it's important to choose wisely in lieu of leaning on who seems to be the obvious choice but will not be the best guide for the journey ahead. You need to be very careful about who you allow into your life because they can literally change the course of your life. The easy choice (or obvious choice) is not always the best candidate as your guide for the journey ahead.

When most people think of choosing a guide, they might envision a process of finding an expert and then making that person their guru. But there are other ways. You may choose a guide for any number of reasons: because you feel a personal connection with that particular teacher, because that person feels like the right path for you, or even because you just want to be around a particular kind of energy. When you choose to work with a guide, it's important to remember it's not about finding someone who's perfect or who has all the answers. It's an ongoing relationship between two people and becoming your own guide is part of the process.

There are so many kinds of guides a person can have. They can be your parent, teacher, peer, partner, trusted advisor/ mentor, professional coach, mentor, or friend. They may become involved in your life and challenge you, asking you questions that allow you to develop a deeper under- standing of yourself. Some points in life may require one guide alone, while other points may require more than one. Be willing to benefit from multiple guides, as they can all share unique insights and perspectives that push you toward success.

When we first begin our journey, we often hyperfocus on getting from point A to point B that we may not realize a lot goes on in between. In fact, it is during this time we must be very careful about the company we keep and the relationships we form.

Like an amplifier, you must connect to the guide properly to make the most of that connection. It is of the utmost importance that when taking on the journey of self-discovery and self-expression, one must be very careful in the company they keep.

There are many different types of guides, but in this chapter I focus less on who the guide is and more on the function of the guide as a core principle of Me Power. Choosing a guide is essential as you master excellence.

MASTERING EXCELLENCE (ME) POWER

Mastering excellence is about finding your inner calling, choosing to focus on learning, and becoming a master of showcasing your uniqueness to the world. You master what you measure. The Greek word for self-control, or temperance, is *enkrateia*. Its root meaning is "power over oneself" or "self-mastery." Self-control, in its broadest sense, refers to mastery over our passions. It is the virtue that holds our appetites in check, controlling our rational will or regulating our conduct without being duly swayed by sensuous desires. Moderation is a key element of self-control.

In Claude Monet's painting *Impression, Sunrise* the viewer focuses on the vivid orange sun, its reflection shimmering in the water with two boats against a hazy, gray-blue backdrop in the port of Le Havre, France, where Monet grew up.

During my visit to the Musée Marmottan Monet in March 2005, I stood as close as I could to this work, trying to

make sense of how I felt about one of the most prominent paintings of an artistic movement. Severely near-
sighted without my glasses, I took them off and stepped
back an additional three feet. The painting immediately
came to life for me. I saw hues of violet, blue, green, and
gray. I even felt struck by how clear the imagery was,
even though I could not see it very well. Standing close
to and then stepping away from the painting, I noticed
no boundary between the water and the sky. The background blended together and when I put on my glasses
and squinted, I could see two people on the boat.

Imagine my surprise when I learned thirty years after
Impression, Sunrise, Monet battled eye disease and visual
impairment, yet kept painting despite becoming legally
blind by the time of his death. He *kept* painting even
though his sight was severely compromised. Monet's
devotion to painting when he could not see speaks to
the fire that burned within him, propelling him to master his craft and produce quality work no matter what
stood in his way.

Monet enacted the attitude of mastering excellence when
he continued to improve his skills, using an intrinsic
motivation to derive purpose, achievement, and ownership over choices in his life. Monet's life and work offer
valuable lessons for us. His creativity can inspire all of us
to continuously improve in everything we do, master our
individual crafts, and be the best we can be.

How did he become blind?

Not uncommon among those spending years in the sun as landscape artists, cataracts began to blur Monet's vision after the age of seventy. His untreated cataracts significantly impacted the colors hitting his canvas, noted for gentle blues and greens in his earlier work. After 1915, Monet's paintings became more abstract with pronounced red and yellow tones, reflective of vision distortion from cataracts making it harder for him to distinguish blues and purples. As cited by Dr. Anna Gruener in the *British Journal of General Practice*, despite this, he "[preferred] to make the most of [his] poor sight and [would] even give up painting if necessary, but at least be able to see a little of these things that [he] loved."

Embracing this barrier, Monet accepted and appreciated what he could about his new limitations. Motivated to excel in his craft, he created an ordered color wheel on his palette to avoid choosing the wrong colors. Scientists estimate humans can distinguish up to ten million different colors. But Monet's most precious instruments were severely compromised by untreated cataracts blocking light and clouding his eyes.

The doctors recommended Monet get his eyes fixed because they were failing. He was unsure if he should get the surgery. He didn't like what had happened to some of his friends when they had it done. Two of his contemporaries had cataract surgery, and because ophthalmology did not have the technological advancements we have today, their eyesight deteriorated after their operations. They never painted again.

After years of complaining "colors no longer had the same intensity," he was finally coaxed into surgery by his friend, Georges Clemenceau, a famous practicing physician and twice-elected French prime minister, known internationally for leading France through the end of World War I.

Lead out of fear, Monet chose the surgery, but he was frustrated with the slow pace at which his vision improved afterward. Clemenceau wrote encouraging letters to Monet, reminding him the surgery provided much-needed relief and recovery would take some time. At his most challenging times, Monet took a knife and slashed his paintings, ripping shreds of canvas to destroy his work. Many of the slashed and sometimes burned pieces were from his collection of hundreds of water lilies.

His eyesight temporarily improved but worsened over time. Explaining his process for mastering excellence, Monet wrote, "I planted my water lilies for fun when I saw all of a sudden that my pond had become enchanted. I seized my palette. Since then, I have had no other model." Over the course of thirty years, Monet painted and then repainted, to replace the ones he destroyed, more than 250 canvases of water lilies. A combination of focus, commitment, and passion guided Monet's attitude of mastering excellence. These elements were deeply personal yet interconnected with the social world, his closest friend, and the environment in which he lived.

Monet drew inspiration from his home garden in Giverny, France. An avid horticulturist, Monet called his garden his "most beautiful masterpiece." Before painting, he planted and waited for the water lilies to bloom, known for their display of floating leaves and brightly colored petals. This environment served as inspiration for many of his most famous works, such as *The Water-Lily Pond* and *The Japanese Bridge*. Monet's primary subject was landscape and he often repeated the same motifs in his paintings, both those depicting Giverny and others.

As a close confidant who respected him to the very end, Clemenceau engaged in a coaching relationship with Monet where they were partners in thought-provoking and creative processes, as noted in the many letters they penned to one another over their almost thirty-year friendship. Clemenceau challenged Monet to create a series of paintings, instead of the two he originally wanted to gift to France, as a symbol of peace for the country, which inspired Monet to maximize his potential in a final masterpiece right before he died. Leveraging his political relationships, Clemenceau helped Monet broker a deal where in exchange for eight *Les Nymphéas* or *Water Lilies* murals, Monet was able to keep his work unreleased during his lifetime. Only after Monet's death could the work be displayed at a location he selected. In fact, the government built a pair of rooms at the Musée de l'Orangerie as a permanent home for his paintings, where they hang to this very day.

While the colors were out of Monet's sight, they never left his mind. In his final works, he used larger canvases and painted fewer details. Monet stood in his own power, failing eyesight and all, and shared unique expressions of himself with the world. His early artistic vision and later his failing sight created two art genres: impressionism and modern abstract art. The way in which Monet handled eye disease and visual impairment shows it is not what happens to us but the attitude we take toward adversity that sets us up to flex (Our) Me Power. When we look at Monet's life, we can see he was committed to mastering excellence, using intrinsic motivation to derive purpose, achievement, and ownership over choices in his life.

What if we formally learned how to stand in our own power, like Monet, and unabashedly share it with the world? How could we structure learning environments, within and beyond school, to support the development of (Our) Me Power?

Monet's story is a remarkable testament to Me Power. Emboldened to continue making his mark on the world until he died, Monet did not stop painting even as he became blind. He continuously expressed his true self, committed himself to mastering excellence, and was motivated to excel in unimaginable ways. Monet chose a guide as he sought to master excellence and put his best self forward. No one empowered Monet—not even his champion, Clemenceau. He stood in his power and manifested his own destiny.

GUIDE AS ENCOURAGER
Belief can be a powerful catalyst for action. In addition to believing in yourself, a single person's belief in you can be a game changer, life changer, and lifesaver. It is the difference between starting your own business or

settling for a job that pays the bills. It is the difference between quitting your job to go back to school to pursue your dream career or staying where you are in fear of what might happen if you try something new.

I knew I wanted to obtain a doctorate, but at eighteen years old, I only considered what was possible in California. At Cal State San Marcos, Professor Sue Fellows told me, "You belong at an Ivy League." For the first time, I thought about the possibility of accomplishing that as a goal. The effect was dramatic: it gave me the confidence I needed to consider working toward how to get into one. Once I decided an Ivy League was indeed worth pursuing, I enlisted everyone who would help me. Professor Fellows's belief in the potential I did not yet see in myself set me on the path to pursue a masters in teaching English to speakers of other languages/applied linguistics from Teachers College, Columbia University.

Empowerment is not contingent on others' affirmations or encouragement, but it can add to the power already found within.

Earlier, I mentioned we should not rely on others' encouragement to feel empowered. But that doesn't mean the motivation of a guide cannot benefit the growth of the power found within.

Sometimes the guide can be a person who can see your future self and their perspective can provide value and help you advocate for that future you're constructing.

I turned down a University of California learning institution and opted for Cal State University, San Marcos because the campus was close to San Diego, the classes were small and taught by professors who cared about students, and they offered free laptops to students with Wi-Fi all over campus. For context, dial-up reigned supreme at the time and Wi-Fi access at the local Starbucks was expensive.

One day as I was packing up to leave class, my peer Barbara Jane Sykes shouted at me, "The only one on their laptop and they're looking at porn!" I immediately looked up, shocked that the oldest person in the class called me out for being on my laptop.

"I was taking notes," I explained in my defense, feeling guilty I had been multitasking, working on my final paper and also sending AOL instant messages to friends.

She put her hand on her hips and said, "*Sure* you were."

Professor Fellows laughed, knowing I was super engaged and respectful, having asked her permission to use a laptop and disclosing I might do more than take notes. Other people laughed, too, and I felt like Barbara was making me the butt of her joke.

I quickly packed up my things and ran after her once class ended.

"Hey, Barbara, what's up with you saying that?"

She turned around and asked if I wanted to grab a coffee.

"No way!" I retorted. "I'm super offended by what you said. What's your deal?"

Seeing how upset I was, she let out a deep belly laugh. Every time she tried to answer me, she laughed so hard it was impossible to understand what she said. It disarmed me immediately. After she offered to make amends by buying me a coffee, I sassily informed her I would be getting a large latte with *extra* espresso. We became fast friends despite her efforts to make fun of me.

There's an old adage that says, "If you want to go fast, go alone. If you want to go far, go together." This could not be more true when it comes to your personal evolution and growth. To evolve beyond our current level of consciousness, we need a guide. You can bounce ideas off your guide, gain a different perspective, learn from their experience, and bond with them while receiving emotional support. We can't always go it alone! We should not. We don't have to. The acceleration of Me Power happens with the right guide.

It was not until a year into our friendship, when I was completing my semester abroad in England, that I realized Barbara Sykes was also one of my guides. In our conversations and emails over eighteen years until she died in 2019, I received an invaluable education. We had fun contrasting our differences—she was raised on an avocado grove in Vista and I was raised in the hoods of Lynwood, next to Compton, and Long Beach. She was older than my grandparents and, for someone her age, got a kick out of discussing taboo subjects. She also loved learning from me and positioned herself as a lover of the learning triad of unlearning, learning, and relearning, which helped her stay young at heart.

Choosing a guide has a lot to do with having someone to turn to, to confide in, and to talk to when you feel most uncertain. They're more than a sounding board; they are engaged, asking clarifying questions and sharing on a deep level. Experiences shared by your guide can teach you things you might never have had an opportunity to learn otherwise.

What's really beautiful about the idea of (Our) Me Power is the fact that we're able to share with each other, which gives us an opportunity to evolve in a way we may not be able to do individually. These are two kinds of the main powers we have—me and we. Choosing a guide is fundamental to showcasing (Our) Me Power. When heroes are tested, they are typically supported by a guide.

A guide is also helpful for shifting from a negative to positive mindset. Noticing we get into these negative situations and patterns of behavior helps to increase awareness. Becoming aware of them and beginning some kind of process to change requires an external sounding board.

A guide can be helpful for developing gratitude for who we are and what we have, rather than always focusing on what we don't have.

If you're in a place where you're stuck, you need to have somebody else there to help you move out of it. They should not do it for you or tell you what to do, but they could say something that triggers you into your next level.

I think about how I've evolved personally and how I've grown in my life. There are so many guides—friends, coaches, professional mentors—who have been involved in my life and are very good at challenging me, calling me out, and asking me questions that get me to dig deeper. They're part of my evolution. This is why I think about empowerment as relational, because if we are going to have any kind of evolution or movement through our lives, other people must be involved in some way.

You can do pulse checks with your guide, just like Monet, who used the French Prime Minister as a confidant to help him move beyond what held him back. Monet was afraid and hesitant to get the eye surgery. Yet, he needed to get the surgery to finish his last body of work before he died. If he hadn't, he would have gone blind much sooner and been unable to complete his work. This highlights the importance of having a guide.

In the end, it's up to you whether you want a guide. It's important to remember you can pick and choose who that person might be. And sometimes they might even choose you. But know the emphasis is on the "we" part and not going it alone. Guides are there to help you achieve your goals and overcome obstacles in life.

EVERY HERO HAS A GUIDE—GUIDES HELP YOU OWN ME POWER

The hero's journey is a universal concept that defines an archetype across every culture. Whether it be Odysseus or Neo, the hero's journey is a framework for understanding our purpose and how to obtain meaning in life. It defines who we are as humans and guides us through life's challenges. The hero is not just a character in a story, but also you and me, each of us with the potential for greatness.

The first part of the hero's journey is separation: letting go of what we know and venturing into an unknown world. To free ourselves from what is familiar, we must be willing to let go of our old ways and embrace new methods. We must be willing to cast off old ideas and experiences that no longer serve us to become open to all possibilities. The second part of the hero's journey is initiation: facing challenges and learning lessons that improve our chances in life. To make it through this fraught process with our spirits intact, we must see each challenge as an opportunity to achieve something worthwhile—not as a threat or punishment, but as a chance to learn something new. We must also be ready to face them head on and use every tool at our disposal.

Joseph Campbell used the hero's journey as a comprehensive metaphor for the deep inner journey of transformation that heroes of every era seem to share—a path that leads them through great movements of separation, descent, ordeal, and return. The epic journey would not even be possible without guides. A hero refuses the journey because of fears and insecurities that have surfaced from the call to adventure. The hero is not willing to make changes, preferring the safe haven of the ordinary world. It's not until the hero meets a mentor (e.g., Athena or Morpheus) that they gain confidence, insight, advice, training, or magical gifts to overcome their initial fears and face the threshold of the adventure.

The guide, or the mentor, is a vital part of every hero's journey. Each of these figures helps the hero overcome obstacles and live up to their full potential. It makes sense for our life's journey to have a guide as well: guides are compassionate, objective listeners who can help us see ourselves more clearly and find direction when we feel lost.

THE ULTIMATE FUNCTION OF YOUR GUIDES: A COCREATIVE PARTNERSHIP

The best guides engage in a coaching relationship. Positive psychologists describe coaching as a goal-focused helping relationship, where a coach and a client engage in a cocreative partnership to set personal goals and develop, monitor, evaluate, and modify goal-appropriate activities tailored to the individual's specific needs. Several people have investigated the effectiveness of coaching. In particular, one randomized controlled study stands out. Losch et al. (2016) examined individual coaching, self-coaching, and group coaching to see if any could reduce procrastination. They found individual coaching and group training did. People in the individual coaching group experienced greater satisfaction and goal attainment, while group coaching positively influenced how much knowledge they learned. Participants in the self-coaching group were independent. Without the accountability and social component, they had trouble attaining higher goals. The researchers determined these participants needed coaching support.

Coaches develop people. The word coach is not only a noun but also a verb that focuses on improvement. Coaching is an amazing service to provide, but many don't fully understand what a coach does. A coach is a trained listener. Their job isn't to solve their clients' problems but rather hold space for them, to allow them to find their own solutions and motivate them in the process. A lot of people think coaching is for highly successful people, but it isn't. It can be for anyone looking to improve their life, build better relationships, lose weight, create more money, or increase their confidence. I think everyone needs a coach. When you're at a transition in your life, perhaps a shift toward a vision or goal you've had for a long time, or a shift away from feeling stuck or frustrated, it's always good to have someone there to ask you questions, call you out, and challenge your beliefs. One of the most important things a coach can do is challenge his or her client to take on bigger challenges—to take advantage of opportunities that might seem out of reach at first. Oprah, one of the most powerful women in media with a multi-billion-dollar net worth, relied on Martha Beck for guidance and support in accomplishing just that.

Serena Williams is one of the greatest athletes of all time, one of two tennis players to win four Olympic gold medals and the only American—male or female—to win more than twenty Grand Slams. During her career, Serena Williams battled injuries to stay on the tennis court. Even as a high-performing athlete, Serena had to rely on guides—but not in the way you might think. She's worked with people like Tony Robbins to help her shift her mindset from the toll some of those injuries took on her. Tony Robbins is not an athlete but he's helped some of the highest performing people build the mindset of a champion. Having a guide helped Serena battle inner struggles and put herself in a position to flex her Me Power. The guide helped her tap into her power within, knowing it was inside of her and helping her to reconnect with her drive and passion and move beyond the barriers before her.

In your life, who inspires, supports, and/or encourages you to become a better version of yourself?

FROM PRINCIPLE TO PRACTICE: CHOOSE YOUR GUIDE(S)

A Personal Board of Directors is a personal dream team of individuals you turn to regularly for advice and feedback. While typically used as a strategy for careers, they can be great for life.

First, recall a time that was difficult for you to work through. Next, answer a few questions to brainstorm who you might put on your Board:

1. How did you keep yourself motivated and what motivated you to keep going?

2. Who did you reach out to for support and how did it help you?

3. Who were the people who inspired and encouraged you?

Alisha Wielfaert, author of *Little Failures* and creator of *Wise Women Podcast*, outlines ten different kinds of people to identify as guides. I've adapted the following list from her "Determining Your Personal Board of Directors" worksheet, but feel free to name and create your own. When creating your Board, consider including:

- **Cheerleader:** One of your most trusted advisors, this board member will help you develop and champion you in all things. This board member will encourage you to take more steps forward and help you think and feel positive about where you're at and where you're headed.

- **Mentor:** This person will help you create a plan to get to where you want to go. This is a person who will challenge your thinking and help you envision different from what you've considered before. They openly and honestly share advice about their path, recognizing yours may be different.

- **Professional Coach:** Professional coaches fill different needs at different times in our lives. You might need a fitness coach, career coach, resume coach, life coach, creativity coach, lactation consultant, business coach, writing coach, or editor. These professionals give you expertise and outside knowledge, from a neutral third-party perspective. They can give us the distance we need to see the big picture—to get a better view of where we are when we become lost in the details.

- **Connector:** It's important to have someone on your board who's well connected in your community—someone who can introduce you to the people you need to know.
- **The Naysayer:** This is your truth-telling friend—the one that will say the hard things to you; the one who isn't always rainbows and roses, but what they say (even when we don't want to hear it or it isn't delivered gracefully) is always spot on and what we need to hear. They will help us see our blind spots. You can't only have people on your Board who tell you what you want to hear. Know what's in your heart before you talk to this friend, but at the same time go to them with an open mind and recognize you don't know everything.
- **Sponsor:** This person will be your advocate when you're not around. If they have a seat at the table they will put your name in the hat for the promotion, the grant, or the job. They see you as a rising star and they want to be the one to lift you up.
- **Wellness Advocate:** Someone who reminds you to take care of your mental, emotional, and physical health.
- **Leader in the area you want to grow:** Identify the people who are leaders in an area you want to grow, meet them if you can, or read about them. Make sure you're at the types of tables they sit at or work toward being invited to those tables. It's important to know who you aspire to become.

Once you have a full board room with the names and roles of each person listed, think about who else might be missing from this list. Might you need to add a financial advisor, money manager, lawyer, or wingman to promote each other in reciprocal ways? Add whomever you may have overlooked to the list. Lastly:

- Think about people who inspire you or you admire.
- If they are still alive, add their names and roles to your Personal Board of Directors.
- Answer the questions: What are the qualities in them you want to have in yourself? How can you build these traits within yourself?

CHAPTER 8

RITUALIZE YOUR REFLECTION (YOU ARE MORE THAN ENOUGH)

*Can you remember who you were before
the world told you who you should be?*

—CHARLES BUKOWSKI

Bukowski's question isn't just a philosophical quandary: It's the reason many of us live in pursuit of meaning, in search of purpose, or in search of who we are. Because the true essence of who we are may be buried deep within ourselves. Our core selves are part of our identity but are not always apparent. Our outward personalities surface and dominate but our inner selves are, at times, submerged beneath the surface. It is in this reservoir where they lie buried, under layers of sediment and debris. These aspects of ourselves we have forgotten or repressed could be our greatest treasures. They are what make us unique and interesting and they can only be uncovered when we take the time to dig for what has been deeply buried to survive. But now that we have survived, it is time to recover these parts of ourselves to thrive.

When we discover these facets of ourselves, what do they look like? How do they feel? How can you know if you've recovered these hidden pieces of yourself? To know if your search has been successful, you must ritualize your reflection.

Your reflection is the capacity to clearly see what influences you so you can understand your behaviors and reactions. Ritualizing reflection means regularly looking back on your day, week, year, and even longer periods of time to reflect on your behavior and thinking. This process can help you identify patterns in your life and how you handle certain situations. Ritualize your reflection and you will gain insight into your own patterns as well as opportunities to develop self-knowledge, take principled action in the world, and manifest Me Power.

YOU ARE MORE THAN ENOUGH (ME) POWER

The fifth Me Power principle is Ritualize Your Reflection. The *me* component associated with Ritualize Your Reflection is You Are More than Enough, a belief central to feeling and being empowered. You are enough. Even when the world says you are nothing, worthless, or uncared for, you are enough. This principle emphasizes the idea of more, reflective of what lies beneath the surface and must be brought to the forefront of who you are and how you live. The idea of more than enough reflects a point of view that permits yourself to understand you have what you want and need, without needing to take anything away from anyone else. When you believe there is more than enough, you will feel empowered by the fact that no matter what happens, you will have everything you need. In addition, if someone says something disparaging you can choose to believe you are more than their words indicate.

There's a complexity to the notion of more in that it's best to stop and recognize what we already have. When we take the time to acknowledge our current situation and appreciate the things we have in life, we can begin to appreciate what we have. This allows us to focus on what we want rather than what we do not have. But it is also true we will never be content with what we have if we always search for something more outside of ourselves.

For a lot of people, the idea of "being enough" or even more than enough can seem impossible. As covered in Chapter 5, we constantly struggle to see ourselves in a positive light because of our persistent automatic negative thoughts (ANTs). But it's through regular reflection that you engage in the learning triad of unlearning, learning, and relearning, as Chapter 3 covers in detail. You must unlearn the idea that you're not enough, believe in the idea that you are *more* than enough, and take principled actions that can positively impact the world. You must trust that the world is better because you are in it and that you always have something to offer, even if the only thing you have right now is your willingness to be open, honest, and vulnerable.

You are a machine that runs on thoughts, biologically primed for reflection. You think thousands of thoughts per day and more than half of them are negative, with some researchers noting more than nine out of ten are repeats from the day before. New research into the human brain suggests, "Extrapolating from our observed median transition rate across movie-viewing and rest of about 6.5 transitions/minute, and a recommended sleep time of eight hours, one could estimate over six thousand daily thoughts for healthy adults of a young adult demographic similar to the one used in our analysis." (Tseng & Poppenk, 2020) In the 525,600 minutes that make up a year, we think over two million thoughts!

Everything you think and feel drives the way you show up in your life. How conscious are you of your thoughts? Have you ever taken the time to examine them? What are they made of?

At their most basic level, your feelings reflect a need your body has, such as thirst. Your thoughts, then, are strategies you create to meet those needs. These thoughts lead to choices you make to satisfactorily meet your needs.

Most of us have no idea what our thoughts are made of or where they come from. As a result, our thoughts inaccurately represent who we are as people. If we could learn to control our thinking, then perhaps we could better control the outcomes in our lives. The first step is to become aware that your thoughts drive your behavior.

Next, begin to observe what your thoughts look like so you can begin to recognize them.

To help stay on the right path with your self-reflection, consider asking more "what" questions than "why" questions. "Why" questions can highlight our limitations and stir up negative emotions, while "what" questions help keep us curious and positive about the future. Asking *what* forces us to name our emotions: "Evidence shows that the simple act of translating our emotions into language—versus simply experiencing them—can stop our brains from activating our amygdala, the fight or flight command center, and this, in turn, helps us stay in control." (Eurich, 2017)

There's a lot of new research that shows when we spend time reflecting, we perform better. In call centers, employees who spent fifteen minutes at the end of their day reflecting about lessons learned performed 23 percent better after ten days than those who didn't. A study of commuters in the United Kingdom found a similar result among those who were prompted to use their commute to think about their schedule and plan for their day. They were happier, more productive, and less burned out than people who didn't.

It makes sense: If you reflect on what went well or wrong in your workday, you'll be able to make adjustments in the future and those adjustments will help you be more successful. Reflection can be done before work, reflecting on what has been accomplished and planning for success to come in the day, as well as after work, reflecting on what success was reached and what other progress can be done the next day. Generally, reflecting on what you've learned and how you can improve is an important part of growth. It helps to not only learn from your mistakes but also identifies opportunities for improvement in any life context.

As you go through different stages of your life, you continue to uncover layers of who you are. Phases of life present opportunities for you to develop aspects of who you are. Capturing the reflections of who you were at those moments in time promotes a deeper understanding of these phases. You must then prioritize revisiting the moments and aspects of yourself you may have forgotten. You'll have different life experiences and your expression of self will be different. Ritualizing deep reflection presents an opportunity for the expression of you becoming more of Y.O.U.—*your opportunity* to go all the way *up*.

How will you refine your Me Power with reflection over time?

ALWAYS SEEK (SELF) KNOWLEDGE: RECOGNIZE YOUR CURRENT MINDSET

It's easy to fall into the trap of settling for what we have. We do it every day without even realizing it. We settle for a less than ideal job because it pays the bills. We settle for an unhealthy relationship because it's comfortable. We settle for a life that doesn't fulfill us because we are afraid to change and take risks. These types of thinking can lead to a life that is less than what you deserve. If you want something better, you must commit to asking, seeking self-knowledge, and recognizing your current mindset and changing it so you can discover what more there is for you.

I met Jackie in a clubhouse room at the beginning of 2021 where women shared their life stories. I was struck by her candor in discussing her experiences. When she mentioned her quest to get "more" out of life, I sent her a direct message requesting to interview her for this book.

Jackie started our conversation by sharing she was raped at eighteen years old and wondered, at the time, if there's "more to life than this" because she was so unhappy. She explained, "I had never been with anybody before that." She was depressed and felt her life had little meaning, reflecting, "I was rather unhappy. I didn't even know how unhappy I was—like when your normal is not a great place, then you don't really realize how different things could be." To change her state of mind at the time, Jackie ritualized reflection by journaling and started to create an abundance mindset, which took some time for her to understand what she wanted to do next.

Before the accident, I was always running. I was always doing so many things. And there were times I would lay in bed at night and think, "Am I ever going to slow down?" There was a part of me that really enjoyed the speed and variety of trying different things, traveling, and working really hard. I would fill up a lot of my time, or all of it, with busyness. And yeah, there's a part of me that just wondered, "Would I ever slow down?" because

I wasn't particularly happy. I did not realize this at the time. It took me a while after my accident to realize I was just running from things that had happened to me. I couldn't sit still because I didn't know how with some of the traumas I experienced. And I never learned in school or at home to process emotions in a healthy way. Or, I didn't learn that enough, I suppose."

In her diary entries, Jackie started to notice a pattern of her desires to travel because she "wanted to understand how other people live, because they have to know something I don't if they're happy." In her initial pursuit of something more, she went as far as Antarctica seeking external relief, "without really understanding that [she] had to deal with some things in order to find happiness in myself. You can go looking everywhere for it when it's there in you all along."

After deciding she wanted to travel to Antarctica, Jackie describes working "three jobs for a year to save up money for that trip." After two days at sea, the first time she set foot on Antarctica, Jackie shared:

I had always wanted to go there. And when I finally did, I felt like I'd reached the top, or rather the bottom, of the world. The first time I set foot on Antarctic land was amazing, but nothing prepared me for the overwhelming experience of standing on top of a frozen continent. I had this powerful experience I'll never forget. It was like nothing I'd ever known before—an emotion so intense that it took my breath away. But I didn't know what it was until I got back on the boat. Opening my journal, I wrote down everything that came to mind. And when I was free writing, I kept repeating, "You can't get me down here." I felt like I was finally away from the person who had assaulted me and away from the things that had happened to me. By reflecting in that moment, I realized, "Yeah, I am free." I was free and for the first time in years, I could relax for a minute. I think that's what it felt like—just overwhelmingly free space. I mean, for God's sake, I went to Antarctica and I was still dealing with my shit. That was really telling to me. I thought, "Geez, how much further can I go?" The universe had such a beautiful way of smacking me in the face because it was only a couple weeks later that I fell off the roof. And I started to learn that the only place to go was in. There's no other way! You can't go out far enough. Literally, you can't go far enough. You have to go in. You have to go look inside."

As we see from Jackie's experience of using her journal as a tool for reflection, the regular practice of reflecting helped her change her perspective. After her experience in Antarctica, Jackie explained how she changed her perspective on what "enough" was and how her quest for more was really a defiance against "settling for nothing less" than she deserved. She stood in the energy of her Me Power as she ritualized reflection every day. Jackie shows us how "admitting that you want something more in your life is the first step to starting over, in discovering that something more is for you." (Breathnach, 2000) Jackie also showcases Me Power in motion when she ritualizes her reflection, overcoming an internal barrier caused by someone who violated her humanity.

How can you reflect on who you were in the past to get a better sense of who you are today and who you want to be tomorrow?

THE "WE" INSIDE OF ME POWER'S FIFTH PRINCIPLE

You can accomplish anything you set your mind to, but first, you must believe in yourself and know the most important voice is yours. Once you find the matches and have the inkling to start this "fire," continue to stoke it by finding people who will support you. Sometimes, the fear of getting "burnt" can become stronger than your dreams. If this happens, remember to choose a guide to help you find your way back to the center of your being and hand you extra matches, logs, and water for when you're ready to put the fire out. "You can't start a fire and then complain when it spreads," (Lila Jones, 2022) so it's wise to have a guide on hand when putting out a fire before it becomes uncontrollable, potentially spreading in an unwieldy manner.

The first step is believing in yourself. Then comes acting on that belief. Once you light the fire, it's important for it to continue burning brightly—and for that, it needs fuel! The kindling always changes as we grow and learn more about ourselves as individuals and as part of larger communities, such as our families, friendships, romantic relationships, or work environments. There is also the kindling that lasts—the kind that keeps us warm even when the winds howl through the cracks in the windows and when "the house" itself seems like it might come crashing down. This kind of kindling can take many forms: books we've loved since childhood, songs with lyrics so powerful they made you cry, or people who encourage you and act as a stabilizing force no matter what. All these people and things add depth to our lives and help us strengthen self-knowledge and take principled action in the world.

Before Jackie's trip to Antarctica, she did not travel much for many reasons, which were really excuses based on her fear of the unknown. But when she was able to travel, she felt a sense of freedom because of the chance for her to escape her current life, to connect with a new environment, and reconnect with her innermost desire for the future. It also gave her an opportunity to take a deeper look to find something new about herself, which she used as an inspiration for future travels. Jackie shared that she used her reflections as an opportunity to take a deeper look at her past, current, and future self. It was from this space that she decided she would pursue more travel experiences—this time, not because she was running away from something, but because she loved it. Jackie's major takeaways included gaining a stronger sense of identity, learning to embrace her barriers, and developing newfound confidence in who she was after her first trip to Antarctica.

In May 2009, Jackie booked a one-way flight to Mendoza, Argentina and set off on a journey that would change her life forever. A friend agreed to join her. They met Jackie at an ivy-clad hostel within walking distance of Plaza Independencia, a square with a waterfall where people gather to listen to music, watch live performances, and eat from food carts. On the first night of their stay, Jackie, her friend, and another traveler at the hostel decided to go on the roof and play some music, because, as Jackie said, "A lot of the time, I was pushing boundaries on things. No risk was really too much for me. We decided I'd play the drums while they danced with the fire sticks." The roof was not like the rooftop bars you see today. It had no secure railing or any kind of safety feature.

After playing the drums for some time, Jackie went over to a stack of cinderblocks and to sit on them. She backed up, sat down with her back against the edge, and put her hand on it. The cinderblocks crumbled beneath Jackie's hand and she fell backward off the roof. Falling "fifteen feet, a little less than two stories" onto a driveway, Jackie shattered her wrist and the top of her forearm, broke her face in a couple of places, broke her nose on one side, and blew the orbit of her eye down into her jaw:

> I suffered a traumatic brain injury so I had hemorrhaging in the front, right part, and back left part of my brain. They're not sure, but they think I might have fractured temporal bone because I had vestibular issues like balance and walking. They called an ambulance and took me to the hospital. At the hospital, they did surgery on my wrist without my consent, putting three deck screws through my wrist to try and stabilize it. But in doing so they partially severed the tendon that connects my thumb. They told me they thought I might have a head injury because I had abrasions on my face, but they had no way of assessing it with such

little medical equipment. I'm beyond lucky to have got-
ten through that. Before I could fly back to the United
States, the travel insurance company needed me to be
cleared to fly, to assess my head injury. So they sent me
to a private doctor, an orthopedic surgeon. And when
he put my x-rays up on the little light box I was able to
see what the first doctors had done and how much dam-
age they had done by putting these pins in. And then
he said, "I can't fix your wrist. The only way I know
how to help you is to amputate your hand." I told him,
"Cast me up, I'm going back to New York." I happen to
know a world-class wrist surgeon.

At this point in our interview, I stopped Jackie with a Nate
Dogg-esque "Hold up, wait!" to get the quick backstory.

"I was an aspiring violinist and had torn a ligament in my
wrist years prior, so to fix the ligament, I went to this
very specialized hand and wrist surgeon in New York
City and stayed connected with him in different ways,"
Jackie explained.

I started to reflect on the amazing "coincidence" of Jackie
knowing a wrist surgeon. In today's world of constant
connectivity, surface-level networking is so easy to
accomplish online. We must learn to build relationships
with people by connecting with them beyond transac-
tions. We must learn to connect with people who are
different from us and seek out those connections and
opportunities no matter where they may be found. (Our)
Me Power requires respect for the interconnectedness of
all people, animals, and environments and emphasizes

we are all part of one humanity. Jackie's surgeon was in a position to make a difference in her life at that moment because she had built a relationship with him over time.

I was also reminded of how important it is for us all to give back to others whenever possible. Giving back to others is a cornerstone for living. We all have something valuable that can be given away freely, without taking anything away from us. All of us can enrich the lives of others.

After landing at JFK, Jackie went straight from the airport to the wrist surgeon's office. After pulling her parents aside to express doubts of whether he could fix the botched job on her wrist, he examined Jackie more closely and was more concerned about her face than her wrist. Referred to a craniofacial surgeon for a potential reconstructive plastic surgery, it turned out she and this surgeon had spent time in the same town in Ghana, twenty years apart, among other connections too perfect to be mere coincidences. Because she had an orbital floor blowout, her right eye started to drop. If she did not get it fixed she would have to lose her right eye. Additionally, she had fractures all over her face. She spoke with her insurance company and found out they refused to cover surgery with a plastic surgeon since it was technically elective.

You cannot express Me Power without some sense of "we" or community. For Jackie, the "we" inside of "me" included an incredible care team as well as her parents, who helped to support her through this difficult time. The surgeries

Jackie needed were exhausting and overwhelming. She was accepted into a graduate program at Boston University but had to decline because of healthcare costs and uncertainty about how she would manage everything, let alone pay for it. When she called the craniofacial surgeon to request referrals for someone else to do the surgeries she needed because she could not afford him, he told her, "You made an impression on me. I'd like to do the surgery at no cost." The plastic surgeon completed an entire six-figure reconstructive surgery on Jackie's face, "with titanium mesh holding it together" for free and "his only request was that I send him a postcard when I traveled." It was through building real friendships that Jackie's greatest champions, the two surgeons, learned about her needs, challenges, passions and dreams, all of which helped them better understand how they could support Jackie during her recovery process.

Jackie's story exemplifies (Our) Me Power. She spent the following two years in rehabilitation, physical therapy, vestibular therapy, and neuro rehabilitation after undergoing six more surgeries. Her health journey did not end with the surgeries. She also had her brain injury to navigate as well as postural orthostatic tachycardia syndrome (POTS), which is a blood circulation disorder that affects the "autonomic nervous system—the system that regulates all the things you don't think about, making my heart rate increase rapidly when I'm in an upright position." With POTS, Jackie feels lightheaded when she stands up because her heart rate increases too fast and her blood pressure decreases, resulting in not enough blood circulating in her body. Even with all of these health challenges, by "taking medication, resting better, taking care of myself in terms of nutrition, hydration, managing stress, and sleep," Jackie was eventually able to attend Boston University and complete her master's degree in public health, with concentrations in global health and biostatistics. On top of that, Jackie is back to doing what she loves: traveling the world.

FROM PRINCIPLE TO PRACTICE: RITUALIZE YOUR REFLECTION

Answer the question, "Who am I?" How do you answer the question today? How did you answer the question in the past? Compare your answers. What do you notice?

Answer the following questions:

- What small act of kindness was I once shown that I will never forget?
- What have I given up on?
- What do I love about my life?
- What are three things I'd like to say no to?
- What are three things I'd like to say yes to?

When times of transition bring about different experiences, what you reflected on may no longer be relevant. What you valued in your twenties or thirties may no longer be applicable now. Create a ritual for reflecting at different intervals of your life. For example, ritualize your reflection by taking photographs and writing down thoughts under each picture. Make the ritual personal to reflect on the changes you want to see in yourself.

Create a list of ten defining moments in your life and include a picture of yourself for each of those moments. A defining moment in your life is an occasion when you realized the path you were on changed irreversibly, such as starting a new job or leaving an old one, losing a loved one, traveling somewhere significant, moving to another country, paying off debt, retiring, or having a baby. Reflect on the following: How did you feel at the time? What were your goals? How have your goals evolved? In what ways have you changed? In what ways have you stayed the same?

LET'S ACTIVATE (OUR) ME POWER: WE ARE MORE POWERFUL THAN WE THINK

In a sense, every day is judgment day, and we, through our deeds and words, our silence and speech, are constantly writing in the Book of Life. Light has come into the world, and every man must decide whether he will walk in the light of creative altruism or the darkness of destructive selfishness. This is the judgment. Life's most persistent and urgent question is, "What are you doing for others?"

—DR. MARTIN LUTHER KING JR.

This quote comes from Dr. King's 1960 sermon "Three Dimensions of a Complete Life," where he says, "If life itself is to be complete, it must be three dimensional." I couldn't agree more. I believe what he meant by three dimensions is what I call (Our) Me Power, the true meaning of empowerment. A three-dimensional life with Me Power requires you to consider what happens inside yourself, outside with others, and in the universe.

Think about it: If you look at the world around you in terms of only one dimension (i.e., what happens inside your head), then it's easy to become self-absorbed. Once you add a second dimension (i.e., what happens outside your head in your community), suddenly there are other people involved. When you add a third dimension (i.e., what happens out in the universe), you're forced to confront moral and ethical concerns beyond yourself.

That's why Dr. King called upon all of us to become involved in our communities. It's only through this kind of full-spectrum Me Power activation that we can truly live up to our potential as human beings.

Embedded in his question, "What are you doing for others?" then, is a presumption: You must first address who *you* are before considering how you might help others. It is a prerequisite that you identify and manifest Me Power before you use it to help others by:

1. Embracing Your Barriers, using Motivated Energy to excel;
2. Focusing On Your Strengths as the foundation of My Education, within or beyond school;
3. Speaking for Your Life to express yourself (Myself Expressed) and the multiple versions of self you recreate over the course of your life;
4. Choosing Your Guide(s) as you Master Excellence; and

5. Ritualizing Your Reflection to remember you have and are More than Enough, as long as you are your own standard.

Throughout this book, I answered two major questions: 1) What is true empowerment? and 2) How do people manifest it? I did so by defining Me Power as the answer. Me Power is empowerment.

Me Power is the combination of self-knowledge and principled action, comprising five guiding principles with M.E. standing for:

- Motivated Energy;
- My Education;
- Myself Expressed;
- Mastering Excellence; and
- More than Enough.

Each abbreviation in the *me* acronym represents an aspect of the human experience and encourages you to live by a set of principles and practices unique to you. These five principles provide a framework for understanding empowerment and how you can use it in your self-development practice, benefiting yourself and the world around you. The Me Power Framework (see Figure 1 in Chapter 2) is flexible and inclusive of many theories and practices but is not prescriptive about them.

Knowledge of Self + Principled Action =
Me Power

You are not a single version of yourself. You are not a static being and your identity shifts over time. When it comes to knowledge of self, it's helpful to think about it as a learning triad of unlearning, learning, and relearning. Unlearning refers to the process of letting go of old ideas, beliefs, and behaviors that no longer serve you. Learning refers to the process of acquiring new ideas, beliefs, and behaviors that can better serve you. Relearning refers to the process of returning to old ideas, beliefs, or behaviors that served you but have been lost along the way. In other words, when you relearn things, sometimes the new knowledge you didn't have before will allow you to see the ideas, beliefs, or behaviors from a new perspective or learn them through a different process, due to growth.

There is no one path to empowerment. It's a journey of self-discovery and it begins with you. Your inner strength is like a compass, a guiding light that points the way to your north star. But if you don't look within yourself, how will you know which way to go?

The first step is to recognize you are a being of energy and light—you are your own sun, illuminating an inter-connected path between your past, present, and future selves and others. You must look within to be empowered. Empowerment means you know who you are and you enhance and express Me Power in all aspects of your life.

(Our) Me Power is about the relationship within oneself and that self in relation to the social world. The concept reflects a fundamental truth about our humanity—we all need a sense of belongingness. We cannot build a better world on our own, yet this realization requires a strong understanding of who we are and demands we recognize our shared responsibility in shaping the future.

My hope is that *Me Power* helps you see yourself as an agent of positive change in your world, shifting your thinking from empower to Me Power. Empowerment is a central aspect of how we relate to each other as human beings, but it is rarely defined or properly understood. Built into traditional definitions of the word *empower* is the idea someone else will "empower" us.

Empowerment is not something others give us or take away; it is an active process we choose to engage in. *Me Power*, then, challenges the notion that we need others to empower us. We must construct Me Power from within.

FIVE EMPOWERING, NONNEGOTIABLE PRINCIPLES

This book is the result of twenty years spent working in education combined with extensive investigations into how empowerment works. These insights led to the development of five guiding principles.

The first Me Power principle is Embrace Your Barriers. Barriers are steppingstones on your path to greatness. Embracing setbacks and obstacles is a choice you make to first reevaluate what you experience and to welcome the uncomfortable feelings that accompany cognitive dissonance. Cognitive dissonance happens when you hold the belief that these barriers, which slow you down or attempt to stop you, are for your own good somehow. Sometimes barriers seem like impossible obstacles, but if you use them as props to take you farther than you ever thought possible, then you can step on those stones and stand triumphantly. This principle emphasizes the importance of seeing obstacles as preparation for the unexpected. You may not have a choice in the barriers you encounter, but you do have the power to choose to take advantage of them, seeing them as opportunities instead of obstacles.

The second Me Power principle is Focus On Your Strengths. Beginning with a broad definition of strengths as a combination of our natural talents, inclinations, and values we can see in action, it is paramount to move beyond limitations and barriers by leveraging one's strengths. With assessments, we can identify what our strengths are, which provide much-needed insights into hidden potential deep within us. It is important to identify these strengths and use them to get from where we are now to where we want to be in the future.

The third Me Power principle is Speak for Your Life. It means taking full responsibility for what happens in your life and literally calling it out, speaking life into existence. The way you speak determines the life you live. Therefore, it's important to find your authentic voice and use it to express your ideas, views, and desires in a variety of settings and mediums. Speaking for your life means finding what you want to say, then saying it, with language and/or other forms of expression and honesty, openness, and vulnerability. Speak for Your Life means speaking up for your authentic self, engaging in positive self-talk, and honoring the responsibility that comes with being heard and understood.

The fourth Me Power principle is Choose Your Guide(s). You cannot evolve beyond the level of your present state of consciousness without a guide of some kind. Friends, coaches, and mentors are all guides who may have been involved in your life. They challenge you and call you out, asking questions that allow you to develop a deeper understanding of yourself. Success is not only an individual accomplishment but also a reflection of all those who have helped you over time. Remember you are the hero in your own story. Every hero has a guide. You may need a guide and you may also be someone's guide on their heroic journey.

The fifth Me Power principle is Ritualize Your Reflection(s). As we go through different stages of life, we continue to uncover layers of who we are. Phases of life present opportunities for us to develop aspects of who we are. Capturing the reflections of who you were at those moments in time promotes deeper understanding of these phases. You must then prioritize revisiting the moments and aspects of yourself you may have forgotten. You'll have different lived experiences and your expression of self will be different. Ritualizing deep reflection presents an opportunity for the expression of you becoming more of Y.O.U.—*your opportunity* to go all the way *up*. How will you refine your Me Power over time?

Me Power is not a power passed on to you from someone else or someone that encourages you. It's already in you. You just have to know how to tap into it. By understanding who you are and expressing yourself authentically with principled action, you will manifest Me Power.

THIRTEEN WAYS TO ACTIVATE ME POWER

In this day and age, the old model of education—where you first pursue knowledge outside yourself before developing self-knowledge—is outdated. Self-knowledge is the most important kind of knowledge because it allows us to understand who we are and where we fit into the world around us.

We live in a time where the world changes faster than ever before. This means we must constantly work on ourselves, expanding our knowledge and skills to meet new challenges.

But how do you do that? How do you know what you need to learn and how do you go about learning it?

The answer is simpler than you might think: by knowing yourself.

The genesis of all learning begins with you. It's a common fact that all learning starts with the self, but not many people know how to look at themselves clearly. In today's fast-paced world, the need for reflection and the ability to see one's own strengths has become a lost art. Don't forget that strengths are your greatest asset in any situation. You are special in your very essence.

Here are thirteen ways to activate Me Power:

1. Find where you can put Me Power into action in your life today.
2. Answer the question: Who am I?
3. Learning to unlearn, relearn, and learn again is the basis of self-knowledge. The first step in the learn-unlearn-relearn process is to figure out what we think we know. For one day, take a notebook or a voice recorder with you wherever you go, and as new information comes up, jot it down or talk about it into your phone. Think about what you already know about that subject, then commit to identifying your blind spots—areas where you may have a certain amount of knowledge but still don't really understand the idea, topic, or concept.
4. Answer the question: How will I choose to learn, unlearn, and relearn something today?
5. Write down three adjectives that come to mind when someone else mentions your name. What are the words they use to describe you? Ask five people who know you well to describe you using three adjectives and compare them to your original list. How do these words make you feel? How do the words from others match or diverge from the words you used to describe yourself?
6. Create a running list of how you would like people to remember you and revisit it frequently.

7. Add aromas such as lavender, peppermint, or citrus to create a different atmosphere and activate your reticular activating system as an advantage when Embracing Your Barriers.

8. Identify the weirdest thing about you, an unusual skill or talent, which could also be a benefit to someone else. Share it in a way only you can.

9. Take a free Values in Action (VIA) assessment of your strengths on www.lanysha.com.

10. Answer these questions: What would be the title of your life story? Why?

11. Create a Personal Board of Directors, a dream team of individuals you turn to regularly for advice and feedback.

12. Make a list of trusted guides in your life right now. Decide to expand that list if recent revelations have inspired you to take action on new ideas in your life.

13. Create a list of ten defining moments in your life and include a picture of yourself at each of those moments. A defining moment in your life refers to an occasion when you realize your path changed irreversibly, such as starting a new job or leaving an old one, losing a loved one, traveling somewhere significant, moving to another country, paying off debt, retiring, or having a baby. Reflect on the following: How did you feel at the time? What were your goals? How have your goals evolved? In what ways have you changed? In what ways have you stayed the same?

As you look over these prompts for Me Power activation, you see a progression that begins with definitions and builds to exercises. I hope this information will make it easier for you to better understand and immediately put the Five Principles of Me Power into practice in your life. Take some time to think about what each prompt might mean to you personally, how they might fit into the lives of those around you, and how they might be carried out in practice.

One important thing to remember: These are not just exercises—they're also ways you can begin to shift your thinking about yourself and others in your life.

YOU HAVE ME POWER

Self-knowledge is the gateway to Me Power. In fact, it is with self-knowledge that we understand the dual network of brain and heart functions as a single regulator of the body.

Yet, the heart is the center of all knowledge of self.

When we think about self-knowledge, we tend to think of our brains, designed to interpret data from our senses and create meaning from it. But I want to emphasize the heart, the true master organ in our bodies. Our hearts are what give us the ability to feel joy, sadness, anger, and passion—the full range of human emotions. These emotions propel us through life. Our hearts have their own nervous system that allows them to send impulses directly to other organs and tissues in the body. This means the heart knows what's going on everywhere else in your body—it's *the* wisdom organ!

It beats 101,000 times a day on average and it's the first organ to develop in utero. The heart has been called the seat of emotion, the center of our being, and even the place where God lives. I don't need to tell you that it's a powerful organ. It pumps ten pints of blood through your body every minute, helping to distribute life-sustaining oxygen and nutrients to every cell. It's also responsible for distributing hormones throughout your body, including adrenaline that helps you respond to stress and triggers the fight or flight response. The data collected by the brain through your senses is only as accurate as the information gathered by the heart.

When your brain interprets data from your senses and creates meaning from it—based on past experiences and beliefs—it's important you have a way to correct this interpretation with information from your heart. The two-way communication between the heart and brain keeps us connected with ourselves and each other. This is like a compass inside us that draws us toward our better selves, however we may define ourselves. When we let this heart-centered approach guide us, we can live a life that's truly meaningful to us instead of one based on status, money, or other superficial notions of success.

At the end of January 2022, my husband saved my life after I suffered a sudden cardiac arrest brought on by COVID-pneumonia. My heart stopped beating, and my brain, lungs, and other organs didn't get the blood and oxygen they needed. Cardiac arrest stopped my heart from beating but it didn't stop me from living a full life. According to my hospital discharge papers, I was unconscious for twenty-five to thirty minutes, miraculously surviving the experience with no brain damage. Nearly facing death brought the three dimensions of my life into full view. I'm more highly attuned to the heart than ever before—and more committed than ever to living with an emphasis on (Our) Me Power.

Me Power is a type of power that starts within ourselves. We don't get it from other people or places; instead, we create it and control its flow by the way we think, act, and interact with the world around us. You may feel like you're not in control of your life—that things are happening to you instead of because of you. You may feel like you can't make a change or that your voice doesn't matter. But it does! You have the power to create the life you want. Me Power is how you tap into your inner strength, confidence, and determination to achieve anything you set your mind to. With an evolving knowledge of self and principled action to Embrace Your Barriers, Focus On Your Strengths, Speak for Your Life, Choose Your Guide(s), and Ritualize Your Reflection, nothing will stand in your way.

I believe you have it within yourself to accomplish your goals and live a meaningful, joyful life. No matter what happens or goes on around you, you are in control of your destiny.

You can be more than you are right now. Take steps toward activating those possibilities in your life—to reach your full potential. Activating Me Power is utilizing self-knowledge to make informed choices that will shape who you become from this day forward.

If you resonate with *Me Power*, please pass it on to someone who you think could benefit from its message. Each of us is an integral part of the world and our inner strength affects the people around us as much as they affect us. When you spend time with someone who is energized and invigorated, their contagious enthusiasm will help you activate your Me Power. The positive, high-vibration energy you radiate when you activate (Our) Me Power influences those around you to do the same. Me Power activation is like a chain reaction: One person's energy spreads to others nearby and the process continues until everyone, who combines self-knowledge with principled action, is truly empowered.

As this book comes to a close, reflect on how far you have come and where you will go from here. By tapping into (Our) Me Power, you can change the world.

APPENDIX

ME POWER MINDMAP

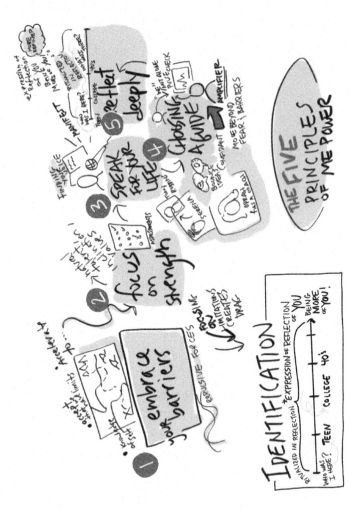

ACKNOWLEDGMENTS

Thank you, dear reader, for investing your time in *Me Power*. I know you could have spent it on anything else and I'm so grateful you chose to spend your time here with me.

This book would not exist without the love of my life, my husband, Dave Foss. On January 29, 2022, he found me unconscious, started performing CPR immediately, and kept my heart going until first responders arrived to shock my heart back into rhythm. Without him and his support throughout this process, I would not be here today. As an amazing friend, husband, and father, he made sure our children were well cared for during my recovery and in those moments when I needed to escape and write to meet deadlines throughout this process. Thank you for being by my side through every triumph, struggle, and challenge to date, including the writing of this book. Your support and encouragement mean everything to me. Our world is better because of you. I love you, Mooshi.

A special thanks to my Nana, Sybil Stanley and Auntie Rochelle Robinson, whose love for me has been an integral part of my life since before I was born. When I first told them I was writing a book, my Nana smiled and nodded approvingly, noting, "It will be an instant bestseller!"

Thank you to my sons, Davidson and Donovan, who motivated me to write by making my writing sessions more engaging. They remind me (Our) Me Power is best experienced in motion—whether by dancing, enjoying life, and/or being present to help others.

I am thankful to my father, Steven Tufuga, who affectionately calls me his "Pilgrimage" and believes in everything I set out to do. His encouragement fills me with warmth and reminds me of the limitless perspective of life I had as a young girl—one that is easy to lose sight of as we grow older. I am thankful to my mother- and father-in-law, Pam and Frank, for supporting me as a daughter.

I want to thank my healthcare providers for the excellent care they gave me, especially Ashley and Brittany. They truly saved my life when I ended up in the ICU and I am forever grateful. I also want to thank my cardiologist, Dr. Alan Ira Schneider, who keeps me full of life with laughter that is better than "all the poison" I need to manage my heart condition. Lastly, I am grateful for my exercise physiologists who always smiled and encouraged me to be strong every week of cardiac rehabilitation.

Krista Jackson, Suzanne DeCayette, Dr. Niousha Moini, Tiffany Largie, Cheryl Boldt, Dr. Cathy Ames Turner, Amy Young, Kristin Kalangis, Dr. Holbrook Mahn, Rebecca

Garcia, Rebecca Kohmescher, Chantal Georges, Maria Anderson, Steve Kidd, Linda McLachlan, Lonnee Rey, and Dr. Eve Hudson deserve credit for the love and support they gave me during this project.

My dear friend and fellow writer Dina S. Paulson provided me with a working mother's dream: a writer's retreat filled with scrumptious treats, strong Greek coffee, and a coworking space in Princeton where I could bring my book manuscript to a close. Her unexpected gift of a manicure and pedicure during a stressful time taught me self-care is best above all things, even with looming deadlines.

I'm grateful for the support of my team, without which I would not have been able to run Edlinguist Solutions and create the space needed to write *Me Power*. Christa Hoegen and Lizz Wangui are two of the best virtual assistants any executive could ask for. Christa kept Edlinguist afloat while I was in the hospital. She juggled several contracts and kept me organized while I was bedridden. Lizz's impeccable attention to detail helped her organize and format all the references in this book. Renita Williams ensures I post regularly on social media and Nina Rubesa supports me by creating a content and marketing plan. I want to acknowledge my personal team of editors, Dr. Katherine Fusco, Dr. Simon Golden, and Michael Jaymes who supported my work with honest feedback, encouragement, and writing expertise. I'm also grateful to every client who entrusts me and my team with coaching or consulting them on a dissertation, master's thesis, research project, or government contract. My gratitude is deep and our partnership is evidence of (Our) Me Power activation.

I would like to thank my encouraging squad of *Me Power* beta readers, who provided valuable feedback on my early drafts and helped me bring this work to completion: India Nixon Lyon, Dr. Lance Newman, Dr. Alyssa Sepinwall, Kristin Bigras, Dr. James A. Godley, Neferteri Strickland, Laurie Baty, Ellen Ahlers, Dr. Brandon Wallace, Christine Moretti, Bob Bathrick, Nicole Stewart, Stefan Tomasi, Aleen Jendian, Pam Foss, Nikki Bartlett, and Jill Laing. Your insights, questions, and edits were invaluable contributions to help me create a better book.

My village of support is deep and wide and my cup overflows with support. My "BlackLinkedIn is Thriving" community and cofounders, Bianca J. Jackson, Melody Rash, Martin L. Pratt, and Kesha Kent, ground, inspire, encourage, and uplift me in ways that make our ancestors proud. I've been blessed to have Minnow Park, Karen Snyder, and Coach Nic as professional coaches and Karen Williams and Diane Starkey as SCORE mentors from the Small Business Association. I want to thank my fellow New Degree Press authors who help me bring the Creator Institute "never write alone" mantra to life: Brian Anderson, Katie Joy Duke, Jeanie Duncan, Somer Hackley, Yujin Kim, J. H. Laing, Richard J. Marks, Precious McCoy, Dilip Ramachandran, Satish Shenoy, Alisha Wielfaert, and Toddchelle Young. They've all been part of my personal Board of Directors and have guided me in ways that greatly influence *Me Power*.

My intellectual companions, Cherida Boyles, Micah Jendian, Lila Jones, Jennifer Olin, and Larry Webb, need special recognition here. Sharing ideas with them rejuvenates my spirit. I love how we often do not even share pleasantries and just jump deep into conversations focused exclusively on the most important matter at hand—our ideas.

Thank you, Eric Koester, for accepting me into the Creator Institute at Georgetown University in September 2020, and to New Degree Press, for helping make this book possible. I would also like to thank Kyra Ann Dawkins and Haley Newlin. I especially want to thank Bianca Myrtil, my marketing and revisions editor, who helped me fine-tune this manuscript with her insightful questions and suggestions.

I'd like to thank everyone who positively impacted my life and supported *Me Power* by giving their time for a personal interview, preordering the book, or helping spread the word. Your support has helped me embed (Our) Me Power in everything I do and your efforts mean more to me than I can express in words.

With gratitude:

ADRIANNA & DARYL MCDONALD
ALEEN & MICAH JENDIAN
ALVIN IRBY
ALYSSA SEPINWALL
ANDREA JONES
ANGELIQUE RAMSINGH

ANN BUSENKELL
ANN LEMING
ASHLEE WILSON
BAYO AKINOLA-ODUSOLA
BENITA GORDON
BETH MARSHDOYLE
BIANCA JACKSON
BOB BATHRICK
BRANDON C.S. WALLACE
BRIDEY FOXX
CARLETTA HURT
CASSANDRA SCHAEG
CATHARINE CAMPBELL
CATHY AMES TURNER
CHERYL BOLDT
CHERYL RICH
CHERYL ZURAWSKI
CHRISTA HOEGEN
CHRISTINA POTTER
CHRISTINE MORETTI
CIARA RIVERA
CINDI DAVIS HARRIS
CRAIG M. CHAVIS JR.
DAN MORRISON
DANIEL AKINOLA-ODUSOLA
DARYLE L. JOHNSON
DAVID FOSS
DAWN FORMO
DEANNA DYKSTRA-LATHROP
DEVYN NIXON
DILIP RAMACHANDRAN
DINA PAULSON

DOROTHY DECAYETTE
ELISSA FRAZIER
ELIZABETH SCHADE
EMILY BURROUGH
ERIC KOESTER
ERIN K. HULSE
EVINGERLEAN HUDSON
FRANK AND PAM FOSS
GALA T. LAWRENCE
HEATHER BOLLES
HILLARY DUVIVIER
HOLBROOK MAHN
HUSSAM AMER
INDIA NIXON
JACQUELINE DECAYETTE & FRANK RAMSINGH
JAIME-JIN LEWIS
JAMES & MIN YOUNG GODLEY
JANICE BREWER
JEANIE DUNCAN
JENNIFER NORTON
JENNIFER OLIN
JENNY SWIFT
JESSYE TALLEY
JILL LAING
JULIE BRYANT
KARMEN ROULAND
KELLY LITTLE
KIRA BREKKE
KRISTA JACKSON
KRISTIN KALANGIS
LAN NGO
LARRY WEBB

LASYLVIA DRAPER

LAUREN R. TAYLOR

LILA JONES

LOLA BAKARE

MARIA ANDERSON

MARIA ESTER & ANTHONY VENEZIA

MARIE CELESTIN

MARIE WIGGINS

MELINDA COWART

MELODY RASH

MISHELLE JURADO

MOLLY CIARDELLI

MONICA BELL

NEFERTERI STRICKLAND

NICHELL HURLEY

NICOLE SCHLESINGER

NIKKI COLE

NIOUSHA MOINI

PAM & FRANK FOSS

RACHEL HOYLES

RAJESH NAYAK

REBECCA GARCIA

REBECCA KOHMESCHER

ROC-UNITED

SARA MULLERT

SARAH KUTCHER

SATISH SHENOY

SAUNDRA KING-LEE

SEKOU SIBY

SHAUN GLAZE

SHIRL RICHARDSON

SIAN LEWIS

SIMON J. GOLDEN
STEPHANIE LEWIS
SUMMER HUFF
SWEA HART
TALIA CARROLL
TESSA BROWN
TODDCHELLE YOUNG
VANOOSHEH RAHIMI
WAYNE TOLES
WILLIAM HEGWOOD
YUJIN KIM
ZOILA ALVAREZ HERNANDEZ

REFERENCES

ME POWER: AN INTRODUCTION

Carnevale, Anthony P., Nicole Smith, and Jeff Strohl. *Recovery: Job Growth and Education Requirements Through 2020*. Washington DC: Georgetown University Center on Education and the Workforce, 2013. Accessed March 16, 2016. https://cew.georgetown.edu/cew-reports/recovery-job-growth-and-education-requirements-through-2020/.

Korn Ferry (Firm). *Future of work: The Global Talent Crunch*. Washington D.C.: Korn Ferry, 2018. Accessed March 1, 2021. https://www.kornferry.com/content/dam/kornferry/docs/pdfs/KF-Future-of-Work-Talent-Crunch-Report.pdf.

CHAPTER 1: EMPOWERMENT IS MISUNDERSTOOD

Bernoff, Josh, and Ted Schadler. "Empowered." *Harvard Business Review*, July - August 2010. https://hbr.org/2010/07/empowered.

Grant, Adam. "How Customers Can Rally Your Troops." *Harvard Business Review,* June 2011. https://hbr.org/2011/06/how-customers-can-rally-your-troops.

Holmes, Elizabeth. "Tweeting Without Fear: How Three Companies Have Built Their Twitter Strategies." *The Wall Street Journal,* Dec 9, 2011. https://www.wsj.com/articles/SB10001424052970204319004577086140865075800.

Jr., Vomhof John. "Best Buy scraps Twelpforce, shifts Twitter support to Geek Squad." *Minneapolis / St. Paul Business Journal,* May 7, 2013. https://www.bizjournals.com/twincities/news/2013/05/07/best-buy-scraps-its-twelpforce.html.

McGhee, Heather. *The Sum of Us: What Racism Costs Everyone and How We Can Prosper Together.* New York: Penguin Random House, 2021.

McGhee, Heather. "The Racial Hoodwink." Interview by Sean Illing. *Vox Magazine,* March 21, 2021. https://www.vox.com/policy-and-politics/22301484/america-racism-the-sum-of-us-heather-mcghee.

Merriam Webster. s.v. "Empowerment." Accessed June 16, 2022. https://www.merriam-webster.com/dictionary/empowerment.

Neisser, Drew. "Twelpforce: Marketing that Isn't Marketing." *FastCompany,* May 18, 2010. https://www.fastcompany.com/1648739/twelpforce-marketing-that-isnt-marketing.

Oxford English Dictionary (OED). s.v. "Empower." Accessed September 1, 2020. https://www.oed.com/.

Rotter, J. B. "Generalized Expectancies for Internal Versus External Control of Reinforcement." *Psychological Monographs* 80, no. 1 (1966): 1-28. https://psycnet.apa.org/doi/10.1037/h0092976.

Rowlands, Jo. "Empowerment Examined." *Development in Practice* 5, no. 2 (1995): 101-107. https://doi.org/10.1080/09614529 51000157074.

CHAPTER 2: (OUR) ME POWER DEFINED

Arnett, Jensen Jeffrey. "The Evidence for Generation We and Against Generation Me." *Emerging Adulthood* 1, no. 1 (2013): 5-10. https://doi.org/10.1177%2F2167696812466842.

Bamford, Tyler. "The Nuremberg Trial and its Legacy." *The National WW2 Museum*. Accessed November 17, 2020. https://www.nationalww2museum.org/war/articles/the-nuremberg-trial-and-its-legacy.

Barragan, Cortes Rodolfo, Rechele Brooks, and Andrew N. Meltzoff. "Altruistic Food Sharing Behavior by Human Infants After a Hunger Manipulation." *Scientific Reports* 10, no. 1 (2020): 1-9. https://doi.org/10.1038/s41598-020-58645-9.

Eurich, Tasha. "Knowing How Others See Us is The Key to Happiness." *The Guardian*, May 14, 2017. https://www.theguardian.com/lifeandstyle/2017/may/14/knowing-how-others-see-us-is-the-key-to-happiness.

Eurich, Tasha. *Insight: The Surprising Truth About How Others See Us, How We See Ourselves, and Why the Answers Matter More Than We Think.* New York: Currency, 2017.

Hamann, Katharina, Felix Warneken, Julia R. Greenberg, and Michael Tomasello. "Collaborations Encourages Equal Sharing in Children but not in Chimpanzees." *Nature* 476, no. 7360 (2011): 328-331. https://doi.org/10.1038/nature10278.

Kersten, Luke. "Convention on the Prevention and Punishment of Genocide." Accessed October 1, 2022. https://eugenicsarchive.ca/discover/tree/532360a0132156674b000256.

Milgram, Stanley. *Obedience to Authority: An Experimental View.* United States: Harper & Row, 1974.

Smartereveryday. "Why You Should Put Your Mask on First (My Brain Without Oxygen.)." July 22, 2016. Video, 10:17. https://www.youtube.com/watch?v=kUfF2MTnqAw.

Stein, Joel. "Millennials: The Me Me Me Generation." *Time Magazine,* May 20, 2013. https://time.com/247/millennials-the-me-me-me-generation/.

Taylor, Bolte Jill. "My Stroke of Insight." Filmed March 2008 in Monterey, CA. TED Video, 18:25. https://www.ted.com/talks/jill_bolte_taylor_my_stroke_of_insight?language=en.

Todd, Michael, and SAGE Publishing. "Mike Tomasello on Becoming Human." Jan 4, 2021. In *Social Science Bites.* Produced by

SAGE Publishing. Podcast, MP3 audio, 23:46. https://player.fm/series/social-science-bites/mike-tomasello-on-becoming-human.

Toland, John. *Adolf Hitler: The Definitive Biography.* New York City: Anchor, 1976.

Tomasello, Michael, and Ivan Gonzalez-Cabrera. "The Role of Ontogeny in the Evolution of Human Cooperation." *Human Nature* 28, no. 3 (2017): 274-288. https://doi.org/10.1007/s12110-017-9291-1.

Twenge, Jean. "How are Generations Named?" *Trend Magazine,* January 26, 2018. https://www.pewtrusts.org/en/trend/archive/winter-2018/how-are-generations-named.

Twenge, M. Jean, Sara Konrath, Joshua D. Foster, W. Keith Campbell, and Brad J. Bushman. "Egos Inflation Over Time: A Cross-temporal Meta-analysis of the Narcissistic Personality Inventory." *Journal of Personality* 76, no. 4 (2008): 875-902. https://doi.org/10.1111/j.1467-6494.2008.00507.x.

Viegas, Jennifer. "Profile of Michael Tomasello," *Proceedings of the National Academy of Sciences* 115, no. 34 (2018): 8466-8468. https://doi.org/10.1073/pnas.1812244115.

Wolfe, Tom. "The 'Me' Decade and the Third Great Awakening." *New York Magazine,* April 8, 2008. https://nymag.com/news/features/45938/.

CHAPTER 3: THE POWER OF KNOWING WHO YOU ARE

Eurich, Tasha. *Insight: The Surprising Truth About How Others See Us, How We See Ourselves, and Why the Answers Matter More Than We Think.* New York: Currency, 2017.

Fullan, Michael, Joanne Quinn, and Joanne McEachen. Deep Learning: Engage the World Change the World. Thousand Oaks: Corwin Press, 2017.

Gruder, David. *The New IQ: How Integrity Intelligence Serves You, Your Relationships, and Our World.* United States: Elite Books, 2008.

Hagura, Nobuhiro, Patrick Haggard, and Jörn Diedrichsen. "Perceptual Decisions are Biased by the Cost to Act." *Elife* 6 (2017): e18422. https://doi.org/10.7554/eLife.18422.

Hipsley, Anna. "Goldfish Three-Second Memory Myth Busted." *Science and Technology.* Feb 19, 2008. https://www.abc.net.au/news/2008-02-19/goldfish-three-second-memory-myth-busted/1046710.

Internet Live Stats. "Google Search Statistics." *Trends and More.* Accessed June 25, 2022. https://www.internet livestats.com/google-search-statistics/.

Jacques, Delors. *Education for Twenty-First Century: Issues and Prospects.* Paris: UNESCO Publishing, 1998. Accessed May 5, 2022. https://unesdoc.unesco.org/ark:/48223/pf0000114766.

Simpson, Aislinn. "Fish's Memories Last For Months, Says Scientist." *The Telegraph*, Jan 7, 2019. https://www.telegraph.co.uk/news/science/science-news/4158477/Fishs-memories-last-for-months-say-scientists.html.

Tarver, Jordan. *You Deserve This Sh!T: Get Unstuck, Find Your Path, and Become the Best Version of Yourself.* Seattle: Amazon Digital Services LLC, 2021.

CHAPTER 4: EMBRACE YOUR BARRIERS (MOTIVATED ENERGY)

Clear, James. "Motivation: The Scientific Guide on How to Get and Stay Motivated." James Clear (blog), Accessed October 1, 2020. https://jamesclear.com/motivation.

Clear, James. *Atomic Habits: An Easy & Proven Way to Build Good Habits & Break Bad Ones.* New York: Penguin Publishing Group, 2018.

Feloni, Richard. "Tony Robbins Breaks Down the 10-minute Exercise He Does Every Morning to Have More Energy." *Insider*, July 26, 2017. https://www.businessinsider.com/tony-robbins-morning-priming-exercise-2017-7.

Levitin, J. Daniel. *The Organized Mind: Thinking Straight in the Age of Information Overload.* New York: Penguin Books Limited, 2015.

Miller, Percy. "Episode 2 | Part One: Percy Miller AKA Master P, Founder and CEO, P. Miller Enterprises." June 7, 2021. In *The Sky's The Limit Forbes Book.* Interview by Dee Brown. Podcast,

MP3 Audio, 24:51. https://forbesbooksaudio.com/episodes/
episode-2-part-one-percy-miller-aka-master-p-founder-and-
ceo-p-miller-enterprises/.

Neff, Kristin. *Self Compassion: Stop Beating Yourself Up and Leave
Insecurity Behind.* Texas: Hodder & Stoughton, 2011.

Neff, Kristin. "Self-Appreciation: The Flip Side of Self-Compassion." *Self-Compassion* (blog). Accessed February 20, 2021.
https://self-compassion.org/self-appreciation-the-flip-side-
of-self-compassio.

Stoltz, Paul G. *Adversity Quotient: Turning Obstacles Into Opportunities.* Canada: John Wiley & Sons Inc., 1997.

Washington, Denzel. Interview by Ed Bradley. *60 Minutes.* Jan
10, 2000. https://www.cbsnews.com/video/denzel/.

Weinstein, Max. "Master P Discusses How He Created The Blueprint For Trap Music, Beef With Pimp C and Why Stealing Ideas Isn't a Problem." *XXL*, May 5, 2016. https://www.
xxlmag.com/master-p-interview-ice-cream-man/?utm_
source=tsmclip&utm_medium=referral.

CHAPTER 5: FOCUS ON YOUR STRENGTHS (MY EDUCATION)

Amen, G. Daniel. *Change Your Brain, Change Your Life: The
Breakthrough Program for Conquering Anxiety, Depression,
Obsessiveness, Lack of Focus, Anger, and Memory Problems.*
New York: Harmony, 2015.

Asplund, Jim, and Adam Hickman. "What We Learned From 25 Million CliftonStrengths Assessments." *Gallup*. April 13, 2021. https://www.gallup.com/cliftonstrengths/en/344669/learned-million-cliftonstrengths-assessments.aspx.

Baldwin, James. "A Talk To Teachers." *Articles*. Accessed December 1, 2020. https://www.zinnedproject.org/materials/baldwin-talk-to-teachers.

Bobrow, Emily. "Haben Girma Is a Trailblazer for the Deaf and Blind." *The Wall Street Journal*, Aug 2, 2019. https://www.wsj.com/amp/articles/deafblind-trailblazer-haben-girma-has-a-vision-of-inclusion-11564761224.

Canfield, Jack. "Daily Affirmation For Success" Jack Canfield (blog), *Self Esteem Seminars, L.P.* Accessed March 1, 2022. https://jackcanfield.com/blog/daily-affirmations/.

Biswas-Diener, Robert, Todd B. Kashdan, and Gurpal Minhas. "A Dynamic Approach to Psychological Strength Development and Intervention." *The Journal of Positive Psychology* 6, no. 2 (2011): 106-118. http://dx.doi.org/10.1080/17439760.2010.545429.

Girma, Haben. "Frequently Asked Questions." *FAQ*. Accessed May 10, 2021. https://habengirma.com/faq/.

Gordon, M. Aquarius. "In Defense of Myers-Briggs. A comprehensive Counter of Anti-MBTI Hype." *Psychology Today*, February 12, 2020. https://www.psychologytoday.com/us/blog/my-brothers-keeper/202002/in-defense-the-myers-briggs.

Lawn, Erin, and Michelle L. McQuaid Mapp. *Your Strengths Blueprint: How to be Engaged, Energized, and Happy at Work.* Albert Park, VIC Australia: Michelle McQuaid Pty Limited, 2014.

Niemiec, M. Ryan, and Robert E. McGrath. *The Power of Character Strengths.* Cincinnati: VIA Institute on Character, 2019.

Peterson, Christopher, and Martin E. P. Seligman. Character Strengths and Virtues: A Handbook and Classification. Washington, D.C.: American Psychological Association and Oxford University Press, Inc., 2004.

Rath, Tom. *Strengths Finder 2.0.* Toronto: Simon and Schuster, 2017.

CHAPTER 6: SPEAK FOR YOUR LIFE (MYSELF EXPRESSED)

Alicke, D. Mark, James C. Braun, Jeffrey E. Glor, M. L. Klotz, Jon, Magee, Heather Sederhoim, Robin Siegel. "Complaining Behavior in Social Interaction." *Personality and Social Psychology Bulletin* 18, no. 3 (1992): 286-295. https://doi.org/10.1177/0146167292183004.

Alimujiang, Aliya, Ashley Wiensch, and Jonathan Boss. "Association Between Life Purpose and Mortality Among US Adults Older Than 50 Years." *Jama Network Open* 2, no. 5 (2019): e194270. https://doi:10.1001/jamanetworkopen.2019.4270.

Covey, R. Stephen. *The 7 Habits of Highly Effective People*. New York: Simon & Schuster, 1989.

Crouter, Richard. *Reinhold Niebuhr on Politics, Religion, and Christian Faith*. New York: Oxford University Press, Inc., 2010.

Daniel, Andrew. *Awaken To Your True Self: Why You're Still Stuck and How To Break Through*. New York: MetaHeal, 2022.

Dispenza, Joe. *Breaking The Habit of Being Yourself: How to Lose Your Mind and Create a New One*. Carlsbad: Hay House, 2012.

Leipzig, Adam. "How to Know Your Life Purpose in 5 Minutes." Filmed August 2016 at TEDxMalibu Conference, Video, 19:11. https://www.youtube.com/watch?v=om-XLTeQee0.

Sterner, Thomas M. *The Practicing Mind: Developing Focus and Discipline in Your Life Master Any Skill or Challenge by Learning to Love the Process*. Novato: New World Library, 2012.

Turner, Ames Cathy. "A Qualitative Study of Formerly Incarcerated African American Men's Experience with Family and Community Reintegration." (Ph.D. diss., Fielding University, 2022).

Whitehead, H. Derek. "Poiesis and Art-Making: A Way of Letting-Be." *Contemporary Aesthetics* 1, no. 1 (2003): 5. http://hdl.handle.net/2027/spo.7523862.0001.005.

World Health Organisation. "CoronaVirus (COVID-19)." Coronavirus disease (COVID-19). Accessed September 27, 2020. https://www.who.int/docs/default-source/coronaviruse/ situation-reports/20200928-weekly-epi-update.pdf.

CHAPTER 7: CHOOSE YOUR GUIDE(S) (MASTER EXCELLENCE)

Gruener, Anna. "The Effect of Cataracts and Cataract Surgery on Claude Monet." British Journal of General Practice 65, no. 634 (2015): 254-255. https://doi.org/10.3399/bjgp15X 684949.

Hughes, Virginia. "Eyeing Impressionism." Smithsonian Magazine, December 6, 2007. https://www.smithsonianmag.com/ science-nature/eyeing-impressionism-180940829/.

Impressionist Arts. "Did Claude Monet Go Blind From Cataracts?" Accessed February 20, 2020. https:// impressionistarts.com/did-claude-monet-go-blind-from-cataracts.

Lloyd, Tara. "The Water Lily Pond of Claude Monet." Singulart Magazine, Oct 18, 2019. https://blog.singulart.com/ en/2019/10/18/the-water-lily-pond-of-claude-monet/.

Losch, Sabine, Eva Traut - Mattausch, Maximilian D. Mühlberger, and Eva Jonas. "Comparing the Effectiveness of Individual Coaching, Self-Coaching, and Group Training: How Leadership Makes the Difference." Frontiers in Psychology 7, (2016): 629. https://doi.org/10.3389/fpsyg.2016. 00629.

Mukamal, Reena. "How Humans See in Color." *Color Vision* (blog), *American Academy of Ophthalmology.* June 8, 2017. https://www.aao.org/eye-health/tips-prevention/how-humans-see-in-color.

Shattuck, Roger. *The Forbidden Experiment: The Story of the Wild Boy of Aveyron.* New York: Kodansha International, 1994.

Sirven, Nicolas, and Thierry Debrand. "Social Participation and Healthy Ageing: An International Comparison Using SHARE Data." *Social Science & Medicine* 67, no. 12 (2008): 2017-2026. https://doi.org/10.1016/j.socscimed.2008.09.056.

Stanford Medicine. "Eye Disease Gave Great Painters a Different Vision of Their Work, Stanford Researcher says." Stanford Medicine press release, April 10, 2007. https://med.stanford.edu/news/all-news/2007/04/eye-disease-gave-great-painters-a-different-vision-of-their-work-stanford-researcher-says.html.

White, Tracie. "Eye Disease Changed Great Painters' Vision of Their Work Later in Their Lives." *Stanford Report.* April 11, 2007. https://news.stanford.edu/news/2007/april11/med-optart-041107.html.

CHAPTER 8: RITUALIZE YOUR REFLECTION (YOU ARE MORE THAN ENOUGH)

Dapcevich, Madison. "Did NEJM Study Determine a Person's Most Productive Age?" *Fact Checks-Health.* February 16, 2022. https://www.snopes.com/fact-check/nejm-study-most-productive-age/.

Breathnach, Ban Sarah. *Something More: Excavating Your Authentic Self.* New York: Grand Central Publishing, 2000.

Eurich, Tasha. "Knowing How Others See Us is The Key to Happiness." *The Guardian,* May 14, 2017. https://www.theguardian.com/lifeandstyle/2017/may/14/knowing-how-others-see-us-is-the-key-to-happiness.

Eurich, Tasha. *Insight: The Surprising Truth About How Others See Us, How We See Ourselves, and Why the Answers Matter More Than We Think.* New York: Currency, 2017.

Glowing Up. "The Lost Art of Introspection: Why You Must Master Yourself." *Glowing Up (blog),* Accessed November 1, 2019. https://glowingup.org/the-lost-art-of-introspection-why-you-must-master-yourself/.

Levy, Johnson Aaron. *The House Talk.* "The Fam." Aired June 26, 2020, on Fox Soul. https://foxsoul.tv/shows/the-house/.

McLeod, Saul. "Wilhelm Wundt." *Simply Psychology.* Accessed October 1, 2020. https://www.simplypsychology.org/wundt.html.

Stefano, Di Giada, Francesca Gino, Gary P. Pisano, and Bradley R. Staats. "Making Experience Count: The Role of Reflection in Individual Learning." Harvard Business School NOM Unit Working Paper, (2016): 14-093. https://dx.doi.org/10.2139/ssrn.2414478.

Tseng, Julie, and Jordan Poppenk. "Brain Meta-State Transitions Demarcate Thoughts Across Tasks Contexts Exposing the Mental Noise of Trait Neuroticism." *Nature Communications* 11, no 3480 (2020). https://doi.org/10.1038/s41467-020-17255-9.

LET'S ACTIVATE (OUR) ME POWER: WE ARE MORE POWERFUL THAN WE THINK
King, Martin Luther, Clayborne Carson, and Tenisha Hart Armstrong. *The Papers of Martin Luther King, Jr., Volume VI: Advocate of the Social Gospel, September 1948 March 1963.* Vol. 6. Univ of California Press, 1992.

INDEX

Autonomic nervous
   system 195
   see also nervous system
Autonomy 16, 151
Autopilot 23
Avocado grove 171

B
Baby boomers 60
Beck, Martha 176
Behaviors 70, 73-74,
   79, 88, 129, 182, 202
Belgium 146
Bernier, John 37
Best Buy 36-37
Bianchini, Gina 95
Bible 95, 154
Biologically primed 184
   see also DNA
Birthright 77, 85
Black:
   empowerment 31;
   entrepreneurs 94;
   women 139
BlackLinkedIn is Thriving,
   218
   see also community
Blind 70, 74-75, 90,
   101-102, 113, 116, 164,
   168, 173, 179, 207
Blind spots 70, 74-75, 90,
   113, 179, 207

Body-based
   experiences 84
Bolles, Heather 38
Boston 63, 195-196
Boston University 195-196
Bradley, Ed 104
Braille 99, 101-102, 116
Brain 57-58, 63-64, 68-70,
   84, 103-104, 111-112, 123,
   127, 129, 159, 184-185,
   192, 195, 209-211
Breastfeeding pillow 147
British Journal of
   General Practice 165
Brown, Dee 108
Bukowski, Charles 181
Bush, Laura 102

C
Cal State San Marcos
   99-100, 158, 169
California 18, 106, 146, 151,
   169-170
   see also Southern
      California
Calliope Projects 106
Campbell, Joseph 122, 174
Canfield, Jack 155
Cardiac arrest 150, 210,
   216
Castle Park Middle
   School 38